1,000
QUESTIONS
AND
ANSWERS

GOODYEAR

Translation: Kerry Milis, and DPM Services

Picture credits:
Fabbri Archives, S. Baraldi, M. Bighellini, P. Cattaneo, T. Gironi, V. Faggian, A. Fedini, E. Giglioli, A. Picco, G. Pozzi, A. Ripamonti, M. e F. Russo, Studio Pi-Tre, Sun Fog.

1994 Barnes & Noble Books

ISBN 0-88029-376-4

Printed in Italy

10   9   8   7   6   5   4   3

1,000 QUESTIONS
AND
ANSWERS

BARNES
&NOBLE
BOOKS
NEW YORK

THE EARTH AND THE UNIVERSE

PEOPLE AND CIVILIZATIONS

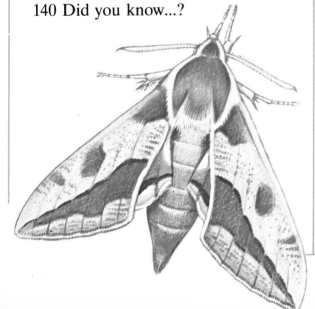

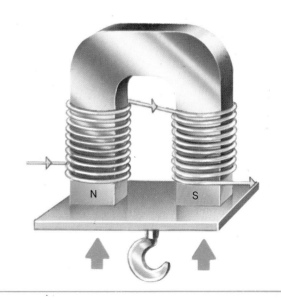

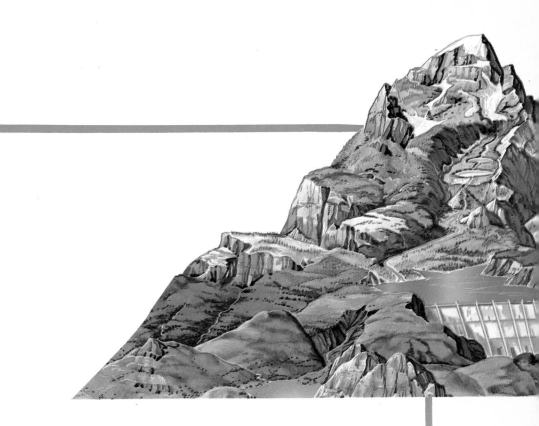

THE EARTH
AND THE
UNIVERSE

DISTANCE OF THE PLANETS FROM THE SUN
(in millions of miles)

Sun

Mercury (36)

Venus (67)

Earth (93)

Mars (141)

Asteroids

Jupiter (483)

Saturn (887)

THE SOLAR SYSTEM

Do bodies other than the sun, the planets and their satellites exist in the solar system?
Yes, other bodies do exist. For instance, found between the orbits of Mars and Jupiter are many small planets called asteroids. There are more than fifty thousand of them but only a few thousand have been classified. They are probably leftover fragments from a planet that never formed. There are also comets with orbits which are difficult to track. Some of these comets are here only temporarily because their orbits take them

beyond our solar system. Finally, there are interstellar clouds of gas and dust, which can become meteors or shooting stars.

Do all the planets have satellites?
Probably not all planets have satellites. At least two planets in our solar system, Mercury and Venus, have no satellites known to man.

Is Saturn the only "ringed" planet?
No. Although Saturn's rings are the most visible, Jupiter also has one ring while Uranus has at least nine. The American spacecrafts, Voyager 1 and 2, have recently visited Saturn. Because of their explorations, we now know that the rings are made up of large numbers of sub-rings, formed from icy

Uranus (1,783) Neptune (2,794) Pluto (3,666)

particles similar to small icebergs. These particles rotate around the planets.

How does a solar eclipse occur?

Just as the earth revolves around the sun, the moon revolves around the earth. Sometimes the moon moves between the earth and the sun. The sun creates its own light but the moon does not. It is an opaque body and when the moon blocks the light of the sun, it casts a shadow. From the earth, this looks like a partial or complete blackout of the sun, depending on the exact positions of the earth, moon and sun at a particular time and how far the moon is from the earth. This varies because the moon's orbit is not a perfect circle. A total eclipse of the sun is visible only from certain places on earth.

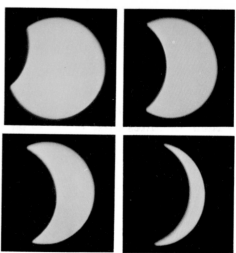

The four phases of an eclipse: The dark silhouette of the moon passes over the face of the sun until it almost completely covers it.

OBSERVING THE SKIES

What is a planetarium?

A planetarium is a place used for studying the night skies. In a large room, a projector, also called a planetarium, projects onto the ceiling images of the night sky and reproduces the real and apparent movement of celestial bodies. The projector (in the center of the drawing below) has two stellar spheres (one for each hemisphere) and projectors for each planet or body to be viewed.

Why can we see Halley's Comet only once every seventy six years?

It is a long period because this comet's orbit around the sun is very long. Sometimes, it is close to the sun, between the orbits of Venus and Mercury but at other times it is thrust beyond the orbit of Neptune. When the comet is far from the sun, it is simply a ball of frozen dust and gases that weakly reflects the light of the sun. When it gets closer to the sun, the gases heat up and produce a kind of fluorescence. With the sun's radiation, the gases and dust begin to disperse. This creates the famous tail. It takes Halley's Comet seventy-six years to complete its full orbit. It is only close to the sun and visible from the earth for a short time. Many spacecraft have been launched to study the comet: the Jupiter space flight, launced in July, 1985, met up with the comet in March, 1986.

Did anyone ever paint Halley's Comet?

In the fourteenth century, the Italian artist, Giotto, painted a comet in "The Adoration of the Magi" in a church in Padua, Italy (see above). The painting suggests that the artist may have seen a comet. It is possible that it was Halley's Comet, for it was visible for six weeks in September and October, 1301. We do not know that Halley's Comet is the one seen in the painting because it was not the only comet visible at the time.

SPACE EXPLORATION

What are spacecraft?

Spacecraft are space vehicles designed to carry instruments and apparatus outside the earth's atmosphere to transmit information back to earth. They can make surveys of physical measurements like pressure and temperature and send pictures back to earth.

Which was the first spacecraft to reach the moon?

In September, 1959, the Soviet Union launched the Luna 2, the first mission to reach the moon. In October, 1959, it sent out the Luna 3. As it orbited the moon, the Luna 3 transmitted pictures of the moon's hidden face for the first time. These pictures were of enormous historical and scientific importance.

Have any spacecraft reached Venus?

Yes, several have reached Venus, including: the American spacecraft, Mariner 2 and Mariner 5 as well as the first eight missions of the Russian Venus program. The American spacecraft, Pioneer Venus, was in orbit around Venus in 1978 and smaller satellites launched from the space craft Venus were sent down to the surface, confirming the high surface temperatures of the planet.

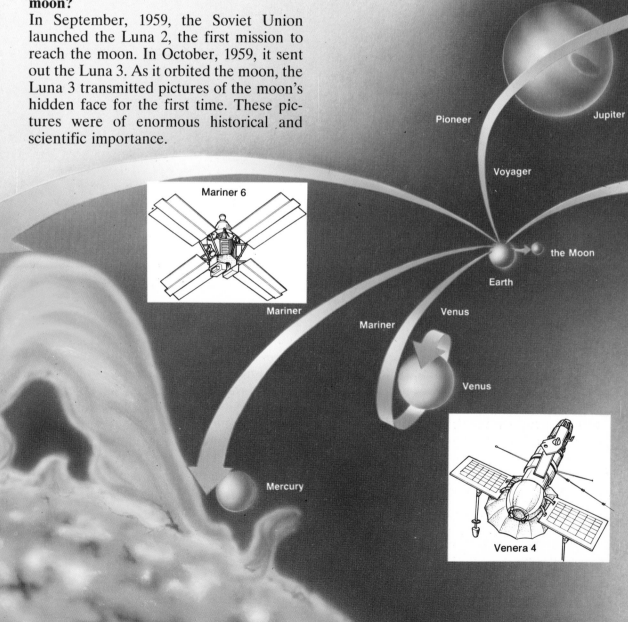

Mariner 6

Pioneer

Jupiter

Voyager

Mariner

Mariner

the Moon

Earth

Venus

Venus

Mercury

Venera 4

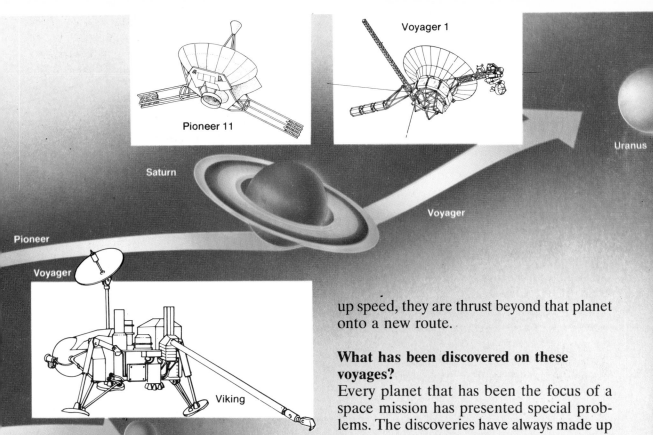

Pioneer 11

Voyager 1

Saturn

Uranus

Pioneer

Voyager

Voyager

Viking

Mars

up speed, they are thrust beyond that planet onto a new route.

What has been discovered on these voyages?

Every planet that has been the focus of a space mission has presented special problems. The discoveries have always made up for the problems encountered. Mercury has revealed the nature of its surface; like the moon, it has no atmosphere. The spacecraft have penetrated the dense atmosphere of Venus and the surface temperature was found to be 860 degrees Fahrenheit. Scientists had hoped to find some trace of life on Mars but found none.

Jupiter and Saturn were explored with television cameras which obtained perfect images of their atmospheres. This also revealed the complex nature of Saturn's rings. When Jupiter was explored, new satellites were discovered. A ring was also discovered around Jupiter and, on one of its satellites, active volcanoes were identified. Even the sun has been approached, but not very closely because its heat is too strong and would destroy the spacecraft.

The transmission of images to earth from millions of miles away demands very sophisticated technology and the use of very powerful batteries aboard the spacecraft.

These are made with radioactive sources of heat and with thermoelectric convertors.

Besides the moon and Venus, what other planets in the solar system have been visited?

The American spacecrafts, Mariner and Mars, reached the planet Mars. Mariner 9 was launched into orbit around Mars in 1971. The Viking mission took two laboratories to the surface of Mars. Mariner 10 came close to Mercury's surface three times. The Pioneer spacecraft were launched towards Jupiter and Saturn. Pioneer 10 and Pioneer 11 flew by Jupiter in 1973 and 1974. Voyager 1 and Voyager 2 encountered Jupiter's system in 1979 and then Voyager 2 continued on toward Uranus and Neptune. On long voyages, the spacecraft take advantage of the "catapult" effect. The spaceships enter a planet's field of gravity and, building

SPACECRAFT: THE SPACE SHUTTLE

How does the Space Shuttle differ from other space vehicles?

The launching of other space vehicles has always ended in the loss of the vector rockets and modules used for lunar exploration. Even the command module, once landed, becomes unusable. The space plane or shuttle is able to return to earth by gliding down to a landing, allowing it to be used more than once.

Is the shuttle an airplane?

The outside of the shuttle resembles an airplane but it is really a space vehicle. Only when it reenters the earth's atmosphere is it similar to an airplane. Actually it is more like a glider plane because it descends without a motor and glides to a halt. This allows it to land on a runway similar to an airport runway. However, the runway for a shuttle must be at least three miles long!

What does the shuttle do?

The shuttle has great flexibility of movement and a great capacity to carry cargo. On each flight it can carry from ten to thirty tons. It can also be serviced and ready to go back out into space within fifteen days of reentry. This characteristic allows us to imagine regular flights into space with space stations or even space-ports for interplanetary flights. The shuttle could be used like a ferry to carry out the regular visits necessary for setting up permanent structures in space.

How is the shuttle launched?

The shuttle is launched vertically, propped up by two lateral solid fuel rockets and a larger central tank containing hydrogen and liquid oxygen. During take-off the two lateral rockets and the three motors of the shuttle are ignited. At a height of about sixty miles above the earth the two rockets are released. They fall into the sea where they are recovered and can be used again immediately. The central tank, however, is abandoned shortly after the shuttle goes into orbit and is lost.

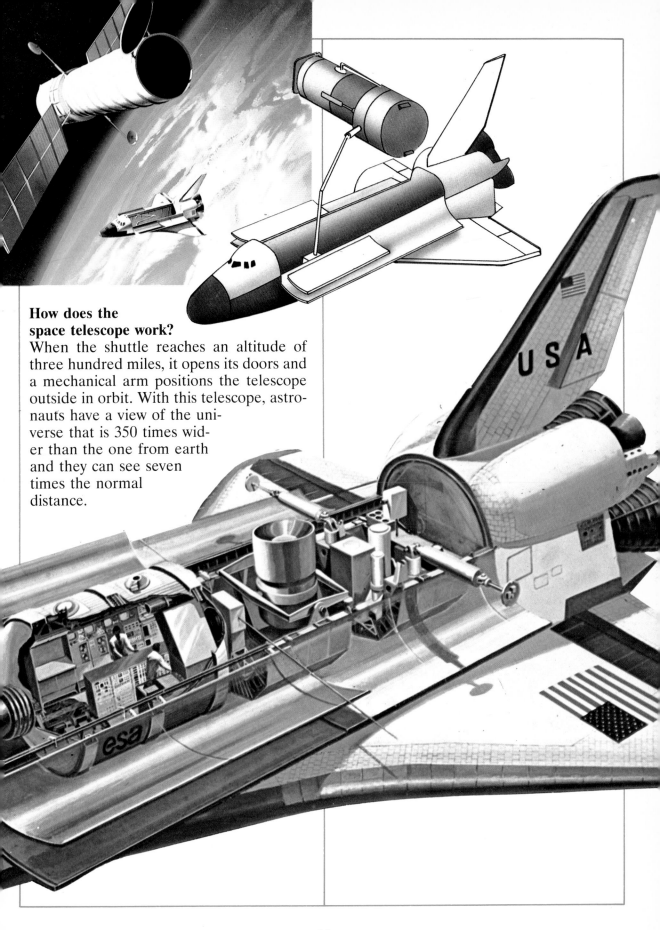

How does the space telescope work?

When the shuttle reaches an altitude of three hundred miles, it opens its doors and a mechanical arm positions the telescope outside in orbit. With this telescope, astronauts have a view of the universe that is 350 times wider than the one from earth and they can see seven times the normal distance.

MAN AND SPACE

When did the first manned spaceflight take place?
The first manned spaceflight took place on April 12, 1961. It was a Soviet mission and the man aboard, Yuri Gagarin, became the first astronaut in history.

When did the first man land on the moon?
Eight years later, on July 21, 1969, an American space mission, Apollo 11, landed on the moon. Aboard it were three men, Neal Armstrong, Edwin E. Aldrin and Michael Collins. The first of the three to set foot on the moon was Armstrong. Five other manned American spaceflights to the moon took place from 1969 to 1974.

How did the astronauts get around on the moon?
During the first exploratory mission on the moon's surface, the astronauts were on foot, but their bulky space suits made it very tiring work. In the last three successful missions (Apollo 15, 16 and 17) in 1971 and 1972, the astronauts had a space vehicle called the Lunar Roving Vehicle to carry them over the moon's surface (pictured below). It was a specially designed vehicle that could ride over obstacles up to one foot high, cross crevices as wide as two-and-one half feet and climb up slopes with angles up to twenty degrees, because of its four wheel drive. Fed by electric batteries, it had a maximum speed of ten miles per hour and a range of forty miles. It weighed four-hundred-fifty pounds and could carry a load of five-hundred-twenty pounds.

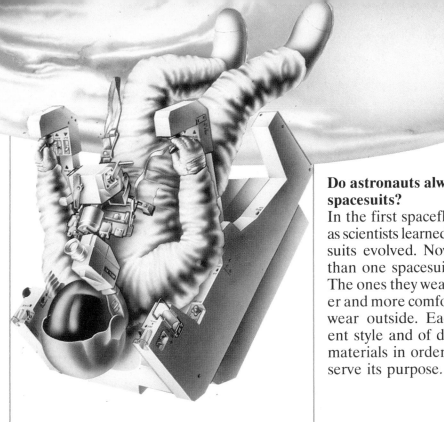

Do astronauts always use the same kind of spacesuits?

In the first spaceflights they did. However, as scientists learned more about space, spacesuits evolved. Now astronauts have more than one spacesuit for their stay in space. The ones they wear inside the ship are looser and more comfortable than the ones they wear outside. Each is made in a different style and of different materials in order to serve its purpose.

Could the astronauts ever leave their space vehicle once it was in flight?

Yes. The first walk in space was made as an experiment by the Soviet astronaut, Leonov, in 1965. The record for space walks goes to Edwin Aldrin who completed three successful space walks during the Gemini mission. These first experimental walks were followed by others whose purpose was to carry out maintenance and control operations. This was especially important for the crew of the Space Shuttle. In the future their main task would be the installation of satellites in orbit, and eventually the construction of permanent space stations and the maintenance at regular intervals of the operations. For extra-vehicular activities, the astronauts could use a comfortable easy-to-guide module like the one pictured above.

Are there directions such as "up" and "down" in space?

For an astronaut in space there is no "up" or "down" because here he will become weightless. When he is so far from the earth, he can no longer feel the pull of the earth's gravity.

THE PLANET EARTH

Is the earth a planet?
A planet is a celestial body that revolves around a star. Because the earth revolves around the sun, it is considered to be a planet. The earth does not give off light of its own but gets its light from a star. In our solar system, the star that gives off light is the sun.

Is the moon a planet, too?
No, the moon is a satellite. Satellites are non-luminous celestial bodies that revolve around a planet instead of a star. Like the earth, other planets in our solar system such as Venus, Mars and Jupiter have satellites. They also move around the sun as they follow the orbit of their planet.

When was the earth "born?"
We do not know for sure. However, today's scientists base their estimates on found rocks. The oldest ones known date back 4.7 billion years. That is probably when the earth was formed. It is thought now that the earth was the result of the condensation of dust and interstellar gases that rotated in a great cloud in space. Part of that cloud formed the sun. The rest went to make up all the other planets and satellites in our solar system.

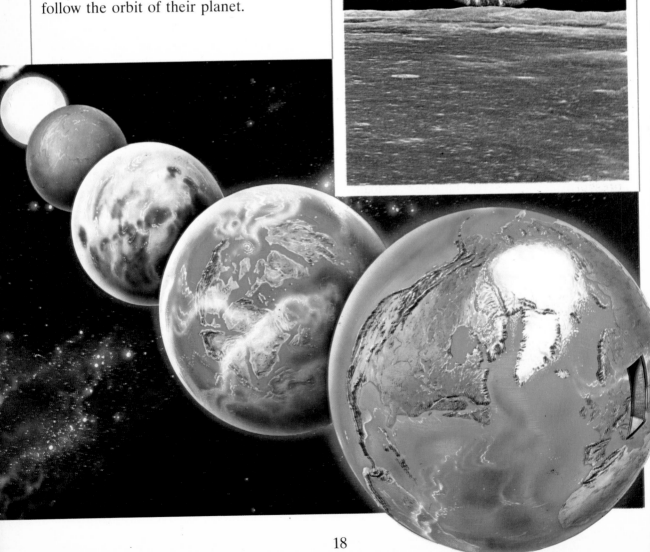

What is the earth's crust?

The crust is the surface of the earth, the part on which we live and the one which we know the most about. It is a kind of skin that can range from six to forty-three miles deep, depending on whether it is made up of oceans, flat lands or mountains. The most exposed part of the earth's crust is largely made up of granite and covered with alluvial sediments and deposits such as rocks, ice and sand. The innermost part of the earth's crust is made of basalt. Between these there is a fluid layer whose composition is of minor importance.

Is it true that at the earth's core, temperatures reach 100,000 degrees Fahrenheit?

The center of the earth is very hot. At the core, the innermost part of the earth, temperatures vary from between 3,600 and 14,500 degrees Fahrenheit. The core, like the crust, is not uniform. The innermost part, more than seven-hundred miles deep, is solid and is surrounded by an external liquid nucleus which has a thickness of more than 1,300 miles. It is made up mostly of iron and nickel. There is another layer on top which is composed mostly of silicon and magnesium, extending down 1,800 miles. Between that layer and the crust are pockets of magma, melted rock mixed with high pressure gas. These are what cause volcanic activities.

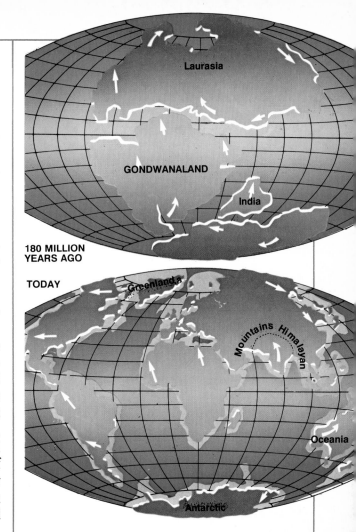

180 MILLION YEARS AGO

TODAY

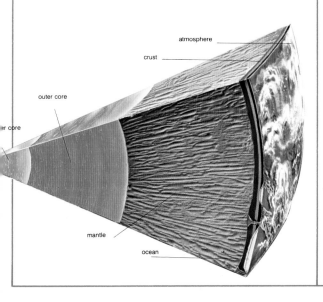

Is it true that the continents are moving?

Yes, the continents are moving. They float like great rafts on the earth's crust, moving closer together or farther away from each other, colliding or being torn apart. Their movement is very slow: they move only fractions of an inch each year. But over millions of years this has caused great changes in the earth's appearance. It seems that over two-hundred million years ago, there was just one large mass of land, called Pangaea, surrounded by one body of water, the Panthalassa. From Pangaea various land masses broke away which form our continents of today. The maps above show what the earth may have looked like sixty-five million years ago and how it looks today. Long ago, South America was attached to Africa, India was an island in the ocean, Australia was part of the Antarctic, and North America was attached to Europe.

19

VOLCANOES

How are volcanoes formed?

Millions of years ago the earth was made of a molten rock called magma. Over thousands of years, the magma has cooled and solidified to form the earth's crust. But the earth is not yet completely cooled. Below the surface, there are cracks that still contain magma. These cracks, or fissures, connect the calm surface with the turbulent interior of the earth and they feed the volcanoes. Each volcano is fed by a reservoir called a magmatic basin or volcanic furnace. The magmatic basin is connected to the surface by a duct or vent. The vent leads to a central crater which may contain secondary and lateral craters. A volcano may be dormant or quiescent, at a fumarolic stage when it emits gases and vapor, in a state of permanent eruption or in violent eruption. The first two phases indicate that the volcano is in a state of exhaustion after an eruption. In the phase of permanent eruption, the volcano constantly emits lava. That phase can be interrupted by more violent eruptions or by periods of rest.

Do underwater volcanoes exist?

The existence of such volcanoes was discovered over a century ago. It happened when the first transatlantic cables were laid between Europe and the United States. It was discovered that the ocean's floor was not just a vast sandy bottom but included whole mountain ranges, some of which are higher than any known on land. There are approximately eighty underwater volcanoes.

Which is the highest underwater volcano?

The largest known underwater or submarine volcano is Mauna Kea in the Hawaiian Islands in the Pacific Ocean. It is over 29,500 feet tall with 13,000 feet of it above water.

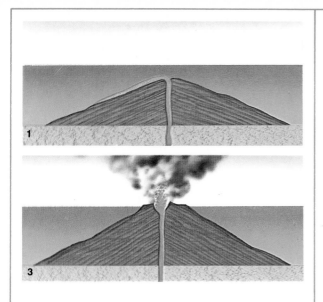

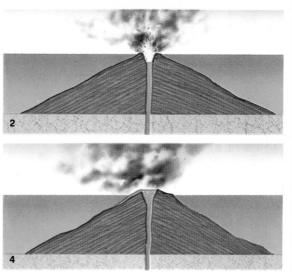

How many volcanoes are there on earth?

There are five hundred known active volcanoes, over half of which are scattered throughout the Pacific Ocean. This zone, made up of the Philippines, Hawaii, Polynesia, the Marianne Islands and others, is sometimes called the "Ring of Fire."

There are also turbulent volcanoes in Mexico and the Lesser Antilles in Central America and in the Andes mountain range, including Peru, Bolivia and southern Chile. Other areas where there is volcanic activity are the Azores and New Zealand. The largest volcano on land is Mount Kilimanjaro, in East Africa. It is about 19,600 feet high.

Can new volcanoes form?

Yes, they can because the earth has not completely cooled down. The drawings above show the birth of the island of Surtsey off the south coast of Iceland, in 1963. Lava erupted from a submarine volcano, accumulated, and built up into a cone. This cone grew and eventually reached the surface of the water to form an island. Each time sea water washed into the volcanic crater of the island, the island was shaken with violent explosions. When the crater was built up enough so that it was completely above the level of the sea, the explosive activity stopped.

Are all eruptions equal?

No, volcanic eruptions are determined by the chemical composition of magma and by temperature. There are various types of volcanoes. The "Hawaiian" has a slow fluid flow of lava. The "Strombolian" has very fluid lava and gives off eruptions of ash and lapilli. The "Volcanic" has a very thick lava flow and also throws off solid material. "Pelean" volcanoes give off explosions and emissions of a burning cloud. "Plinian" volcanoes have old craters which explode and spread rock, lava, ash and lapilli for miles around.

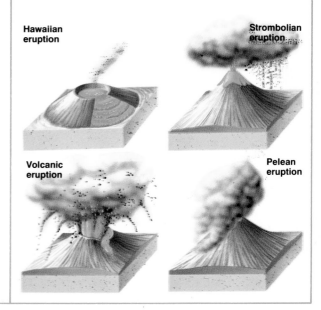

Hawaiian eruption

Strombolian eruption

Volcanic eruption

Pelean eruption

EARTHQUAKES

Why does the earth shake?

If we throw a stone into the water, at the point that it falls in, a series of concentric circles form. At first they are very close and continuous but then they grow farther apart and become thinner. The same thing happens on the earth's surface. A "shock" creates a series of vibrations that produces earthquakes.

Where does this "shock" come from?

The earth's crust is made up of huge plates that float over a molten material, magma. When these plates, moving very slowly, collide, they produce a shock that makes the earth's surface tremble.

What is a "hypocenter?"

It is the point where the plates collide, producing seismic or earthquake waves. This collision occurs beneath the earth's surface.

What are seismic waves?

They are vibrations which, following the collision of the plates, reproduce until they reach the surface. If they move horizontally, they are called "primary" or "compressional" waves. If the vibrations are perpendicular to the direction they are moving in, they are called "secondary" or "transverse" waves.

Do these collisions of plates always produce earthquakes?

If the rocks that are close to the collision are elastic, they absorb the shock and no earthquake is felt. But if the rocks are very hard, they break. When this happens the shock is strong and we feel an earthquake.

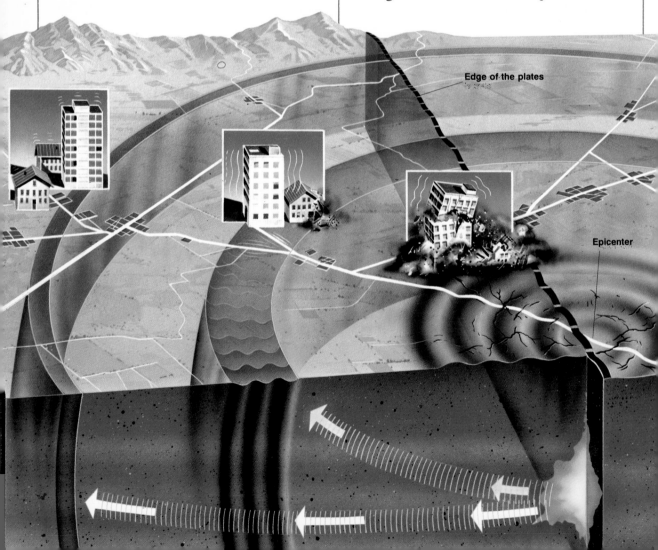

Edge of the plates

Epicenter

Can we measure the vibrations that do not reach the earth's surface?

Very sensitive equipment has been invented, called a seismograph, that can register earthquakes, both mild and catastrophic. They also register the kinds of waves, primary (1) or secondary (2).

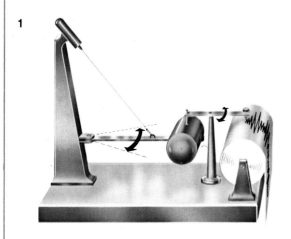

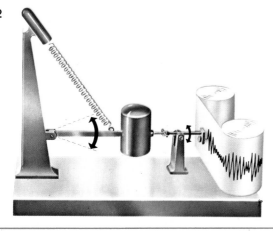

How does a seismograph work?

A moveable pen resting on a roll of paper is attached at the other end to a counterweight. The pen records the vibrations that the machine registers. If there are no vibrations, the line the pen draws is straight. If there is activity, the line drawn is a zig-zag.

How are earthquakes classified?

Scientists have invented two different scales of measurement. One is the Richter scale and the other is the Mercalli. The diagrams registered by the seismograph are given a number, according to the intensity of the shock. For example, a one degree shock on the Richter scale is very mild while the highest registered, nine degrees, is catastrophic, meaning there is total destruction.

Is it possible to prevent earthquakes?

Today it is only possible to predict where an earthquake will happen, but not when or with what intensity. We know from experience that animals are more sensitive than man as to when one will take place. Animals become very agitated a few minutes before an earthquake occurs (see the above drawing). Man has learned to protect himself as well as he can from this natural phenomenon. In zones that are particularly badly hit, like Japan, houses are built of wood and paper. With more advanced technology, buildings are made of a special cement that has a certain amount of elasticity.

MOUNTAINS AND GLACIERS

Does it take long for a mountain to form?
Some mountains such as those formed by volcanoes are "born" and begin to grow in only a few days. Otherwise it is a slow, complicated process.

How are mountains formed?
The continents are slowly but continuously moving. For example, North America moves two to four inches away from Europe and Africa each year. Continents are like enormous rafts floating over the layer of molten rock which makes up the core of the earth. Sometimes they get closer and sometimes they move apart. When two continents collide, the layers of rock buckle and overlap (see illustration below). The point where they collide fuses together over a very long time and a mountain range is formed.

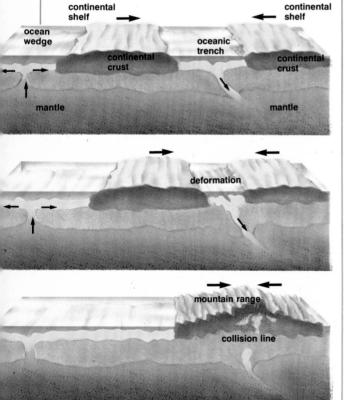

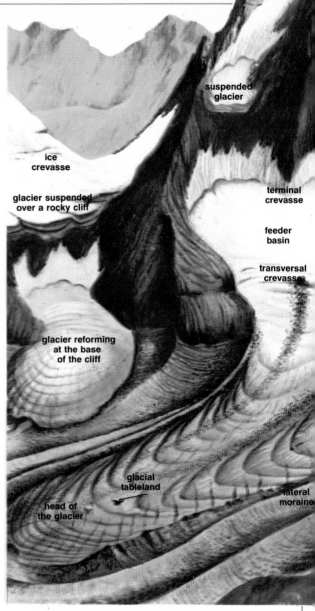

Are all mountains alike?
The surface of the earth is constantly changing. It is shaped by wind and rain and altered by periods of heat and cold. Affected over thousands of years by the corrosive action of the atmosphere, even mountains change. Sharp peaks are worn down and rounded, and the sides become smooth. Rivers and glaciers carve out deep valleys. Narrow rivers form V-shaped valleys while glaciers, which are wider and thicker, carve out U-shapes.

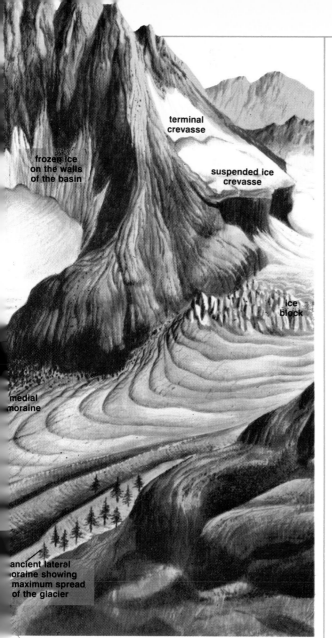

terminal crevasse

frozen ice on the walls of the basin

suspended ice crevasse

ice block

medial moraine

ancient lateral moraine showing maximum spread of the glacier

Do glaciers move?

Yes, glaciers move, but they do so very slowly, almost like melting wax. Gravity may pull them down the steep slopes where they were formed. Sometimes the weight of the ice itself moves them. As a glacier slides down towards the valley floor, friction, from direct contact with the rocks underneath it, melts some of the ice. This helps it to move along. When it reaches a more temperate climate, the warmer weather melts the snow on the glacier's surface. This melted snow forms small waterfalls that empty their water into the main stream of a river.

What is a moraine?

As a glacier moves slowly over the ground, it breaks down the rocky mountain walls and picks up and carries along rubble and debris. This debris is eventually deposited at the bottom of the glacier. When the glacier melts, the debris is left behind and forms a long ridge called a moraine.

LONGITUDINAL SECTION

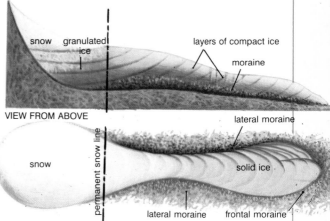

snow   granulated ice

layers of compact ice

moraine

VIEW FROM ABOVE

lateral moraine

snow

permanent snow line

solid ice

lateral moraine   frontal moraine

How are glaciers formed?

Every year an enormous amount of snow falls in the highest altitudes. Because of the very cold temperatures, it freezes. Even when spring arrives, it is not warm enough in these places to melt all of the ice. Glaciers are "born" in zones above the snow line where snow does not melt.

Where are glaciers formed?

They are typically "born" in a hollow rocky area of a mountain. These hollows have a characteristic basin shape, with steep rocky walls where snow can collect.

Are there glaciers in America?

Along the west coast, in Alaska, Washington, Oregon and California there are many glaciers. Glacier National Park in Montana has nearly fifty glaciers. Alaska's Hubbard Glacier is one of the longest alpine glaciers in the world.

FOSSILS

What are fossils?

Fossils are the remains of ancient plants and animals that have been preserved intact. Usually when an animal or plant dies, its body is broken down by organisms in the air. But if it is covered by sediment, the hard parts, such as the skeleton, become preserved. If the sediment then turns into rock and the rock does not change very much, the remains could survive for millions of years. What remains is called a fossil.

Are petrified forests fossils?

Yes. In this case, fossilization came about through "mineralization," a process where mineral substances replace organic ones. The most famous petrified forest is in Arizona. It has petrified tree trunks that are over two-hundred million years old.

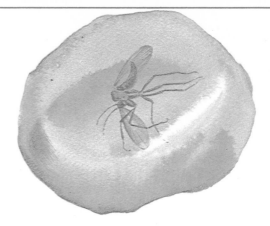

What are "trilobites?"

They are fossilized animals, marine arthropods, which were very common during the Paleozoic, or Ancient, era from five hundred fifty to two hundred seventy five million years ago. They were given this name because their carapace, or external shell, was divided into three parts or lobes. The two examples shown above are typical of a curious process of fossilization. Certain objects that had been buried were later completely destroyed by the infiltration of subterranean water. Left behind was a space in the stone that exactly matched the original shape of the object, almost like a print. Later new sediment filled up this cavity to produce a hard cast of the object.

Are trilobites the oldest fossils?

No, the oldest fossils, algae and bacteria, are three billion years older. They were found in the region around Lake Superior in North America, in the Transvaal in South Africa and in Australia.

Have fossils of reptiles been found?

Yes, reptilian fossils have been found in North America and in Africa. They appeared on earth in the Permian period, two hundred eighty to two hundred twenty five million years ago, a time which may have looked something like the drawing on the opposite page. The reptiles in the drawing are of the Pelicosaurus family from which the first mammals came.

Do insect fossils also exist?

Yes, an example of one is in the above drawing. It is an insect trapped in amber and was discovered in Germany. It belongs to the Oligocene period, dating back twenty-six to twenty-seven million years ago.

How can you tell the age of a fossil?

Determing the age of a fossil is a very complicated process and different methods are used to find out different things. For example, new layers of rocks form on top of older ones. These layers can be analyzed to give relative dates, based on their relationship to each other and to organisms and climatic events. The most important method used is absolute dating, which can tell us the age of something in years. Absolute dating determines the residual radioactivity of the object whose age we want to know. Both fossils and rocks contain radioactive atoms. Over time, these atoms disintegrate, producing non-radioactive isotopes. Scientists know the period of time over which a given quantity of radioactive atoms is reduced by decay, giving rise to the relative isotopes. They can then estimate fairly reliably the age of a sample. Some radioactive atoms are carbon 14, uranium, thorium, rubidium and potassium 40.

ROCKS

What is mineralogy?
It is the study of minerals and their structure, through the analysis of their physical, chemical and optical properties. The rocks on our planet are all made of minerals.

Do rocks last forever?
If we look at the rocky sides of a mountain, they seem very solid, hard and consistent. But rocks had a beginning too, and they live and die like everything else in nature. Made up of all different kinds of minerals, rocks have life cycles that are played out over millions of years.

How did rock form in the beginning?
When our planet was formed, there was a mass of molten material that slowly cooled on the surface of the earth. Rock was formed as a result of that cooling.

Are there different kinds of rock?
Just like the animal and vegetable world has different species, rocks have their own characteristics, too. These vary depending on what happened to them after the initial cooling period. Rocks can be classified as metamorphic, sedimentary, eruptive and magmatic. If you look at the illustration below, you can see some of the places they came from.

What are metamorphic rocks?
They are rocks which underwent a series of sudden changes in their structure. This created a kind of metamorphosis that replaced the original characteristics with others that were different. Marble for example, was originally made of limestone, a coal anthracite.

How did such changes happen?
They are the result of one of three factors: heat, pressure or a chemical reaction. Sudden high temperatures on the earth's surface can alter rock. When mountains form, they may be subjected to enormous pressure, followed by blows from the continental plates. Hot water, steam or gas leaking into the structure of a rock can produce an infinite series of chemical reactions. Shown above is an example of a metamorphic rock, limestone schist.

subterranean volcano

seabed

andesite

mica-schist

What are sedimentary rocks?

Sediment that has eroded from the land is carried by streams and accumulates at the bottom of the sea. Because of the continuous flow of the streams, new sediment is always arriving to cover up the old and eventually many layers build up. Constant pressure eventually mixes and hardens the material creating sedimentary rock. The different layers are in fact the most visible characteristic of this kind of rock (see the above picture).

How long does it take for sedimentary rock to form?

There are approximate calculations that range from four to five hundred years for the creation of sandstone to more than two thousand for limestone to form a twelve-inch layer.

What are volcanic rocks?

When a volcano is active, it shoots out molten material. Once this material contacts the surface of the earth, it cools and solidifies, forming volcanic or igneous rock.

Are such rocks formed only by volcanic eruptions?

No. At times, magma, which is melted rock inside the earth, flows slowly toward the surface, carrying with it or melting other rocks that make up the earth's crust. If they are not thrown out of the earth violently, they end up cooling near the earth's surface. They form an igneous rock called "intrusive," while those formed from volcanic eruptions are called "extrusive." In the above picture you can see basalt formed by the eruption of a volcano.

tremolite

sandstone

granite

tufa

THE SEA AND THE SEACOAST

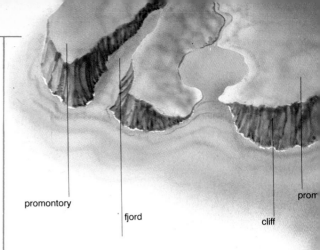

promontory
fjord
cliff
prom

How does the sea affect the land?

The sea has always been an object of fascination for man and an incomparable source of life. The oldest civilizations in the world developed along its coasts, which equal about 280,000 miles in length. There they took advantage of the extraordinary resources the sea offered and the temperate effect it had on the climate. Over millions of years, the sea has modified the coastline, eroding it here and adding on to it there with sediment carried by rivers. The coastline in fact is constantly changing and taking on new forms (see the illustrations below). This happens because of the action of the tides, daily variations in the movement of water that are linked to the positions of the sun and moon, currents, waves, the wind and changing sea levels.

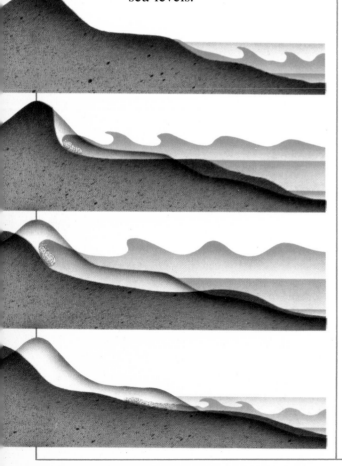

How are dunes formed?

Dunes are formed when sand builds up against some obstacle. There are dunes in the desert, formed by wind storms, and there are dunes along the seacoast, formed by the movement of the sea (see the illustrations below, left). Sometimes when the sea dries up, the dunes harden and become fossilized.

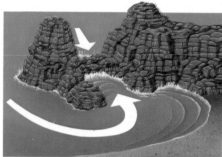

How are tall rock columns in the sea formed?

In the sequence of three illustrations above, you can see how such rock columns are formed. The motion of the waves, determined by the shape of the coast, is strongest against the weakest and most exposed parts of the rocks. Over time, slow erosion breaks off a fragment and it remains isolated from the rest. These formations are rather common and are characteristic of certain coastlines. Two places with famous rock columns are the Isle of Capri in Italy and the Isle of Wight in England.

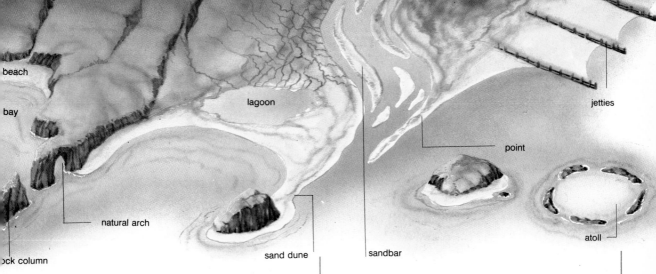

beach

bay

lagoon

natural arch

ock column

sand dune

sandbar

point

jetties

atoll

How are beaches formed?

Beaches are made by deposits of pebbles, shells or sand from the sea. These form a sloping strip of land along the edge of the sea. The fine grains of sand can be white, pink, black or even greenish, depending on what kind of mineral they are made of. Sand is used to make mortar and in the manufacturing of glass and ceramics.

How does man protect himself from the erosive action of the sea?

There are various ways in which this can be done. Marine dikes defend the coast from the impact of the waves. Breakwaters, which are artificial barriers, break the impact of the waves by limiting their force. Jetties, which are long perpendicular arms along the coast, act as brakes for the current and aid in the growth of beaches.

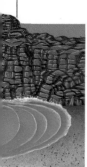 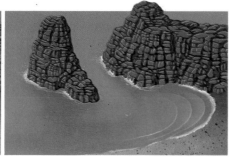

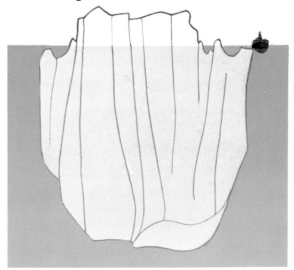

What kinds of coastlines are there?

Coastline means the line that separates the land from the sea. There are two basic types of coastline. One kind is steep and rocky. It is characterized by cliffs that rise straight up from the sea or by deep and narrow indentations in the land called fjords. Fjords are commonly found in Scandinavia. The other kind of coastline is low, and is usually either icy or sandy. It is formed by the slow progressive accumulation of debris and small rocks. Coral reefs are a kind of low rocky coastline formed by debris and coral banks.

What is an iceberg?

It is a mountain of ice floating in the sea. A small part of it, about one-ninth, is above the surface of the water, while the rest is under water. Broken off from the polar ice caps by the effect of the action of the sea, it drifts along, pushed by the wind and the current. Icebergs can be a dangerous threat to nearby ships.

DEEP-SEA FISHING

Where are the best places for deep-sea fishing?

The biggest areas for commercial deep-sea fishing are usually found where ocean currents meet or separate. The turbulence created brings up cold water rich in mineral salts. The best fishing areas often can be found in water no deeper than 1,150 feet. In North America they are found along the Grand Banks off of Canada, the Georges Bank off of New England and in the Gulf of Alaska on the west coast.

Is deep-sea fishing an important activity?

Yes. By now it has become an industrialized activity important as a source of food and income for many countries.

Can fishing boats catch and process fish?

In the past, once fish were caught, the fishermen had to return immediately to port with their precious cargo. Today ocean-going fishing boats, some of them more than three-hundred feet long, have refrigerated holds that can preserve the fish (by refrigeration, freezing and packing), as well as process and prepare them. This allows the fishermen to stay out at sea for long periods.

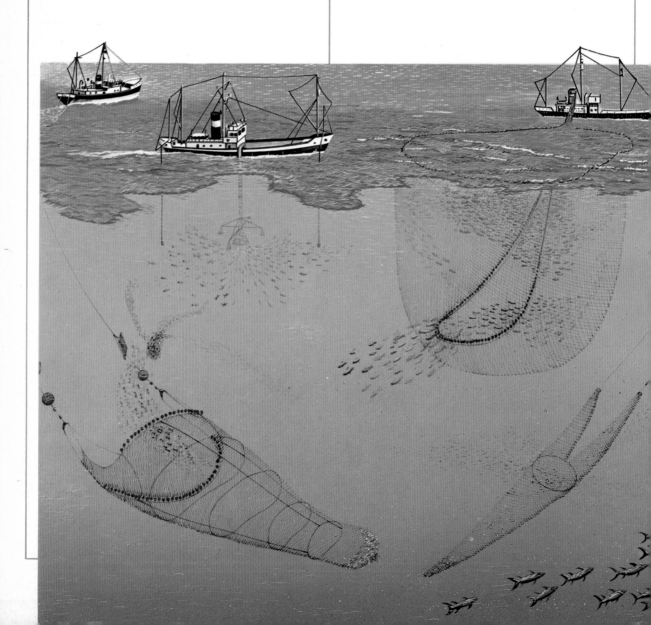

Are there many different kinds of deep-sea fishing?

Yes, and almost all of them require special vessels. The most important methods are shown in the drawing below. From left to right they include: trawling for fish, where a net is dragged along the bottom of the ocean (although it produces a huge catch of fish, this method can ruin the floor of the ocean); fishing with electric currents (an electric field created by immersed electrodes pushes the fish towards a pump which sucks them up onto the boat); fishing with a closed net; fishing with a trawling net; fishing with a drag-net (a net is hung vertically in the water and captures the fish that try to pass through it); fishing with echo-sound; and fishing with artificial satellites to identify shoals of fish.

How are tuna caught?

Pelagic fish like swordfish and tuna are usually caught with long lines with baited fish-hooks attached.

These are hung from deep-sea fishing boats over vast areas. The Japanese "long-liners" that work in the Indian Ocean have lines some thirty miles long. Usually tuna is processed aboard ship.

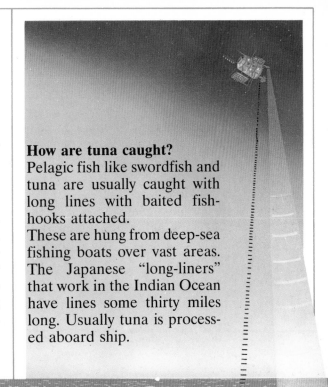

RIVERS

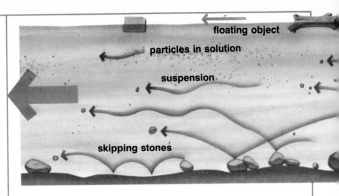

floating object
particles in solution
suspension
skipping stones

What is a river basin?
Water is collected over a wide area from creeks, brooks, streams and small rivers to form a larger river. The area around that river is called the river basin.

What determines the behavior of a river?
The most important factor is the amount of precipitation in the atmosphere, which falls in the form of rain or heavy snow in the mountains. When winter snows melt in the spring, they supply the river with a great deal of water. Precipitation can influence both how deep the river is and how fast it flows. Sometimes the flow of water is both unexpected and very strong and the river overflows it banks. This can cause damage to the surrounding area.

Can a river affect the landscape?
Yes, it can. A river is a very powerful natural force. Over the centuries, a river will gradually cut a path through the land. Eventually this creates a valley through which the river flows.

Do rivers erode the land?
At the source of a river, water erodes the rocky ground over which it travels. Large stones and debris are carried by the current and crash against the rocks they pass over (see the above left illustration). This increases the erosive force of the river and breaks down more rock. With fewer obstacles in its path, the river flows more quickly until it reaches flatter lands. Then, the process reverses and the water begins to deposit the sediment it has picked up.

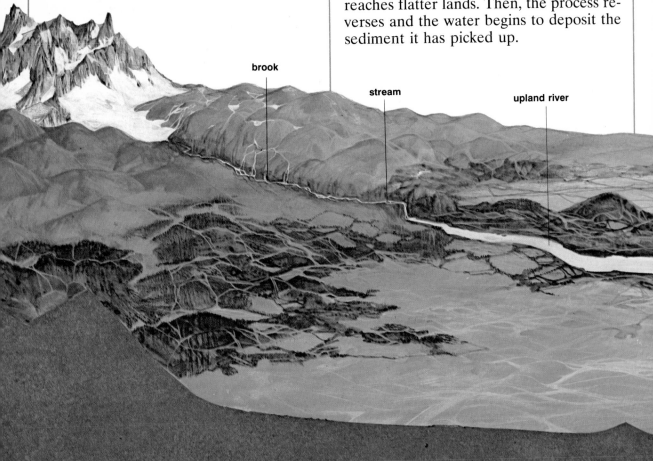

brook

stream

upland river

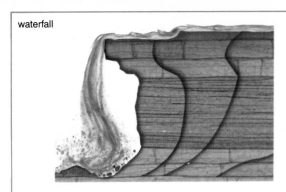
waterfall

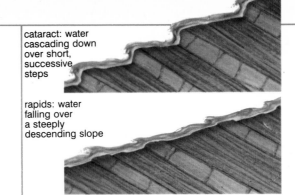
cataract: water cascading down over short, successive steps

rapids: water falling over a steeply descending slope

What is sedimentation?

It is the opposite of erosion, the gradual wearing away of something. Debris, called "sediment," is torn from rocks upstream and carried by the strong current down through the mountains. When the river reaches the plains lying at the base of the mountain chain, it leaves behind some of this debris. The river continues to carry small light deposits until it reaches the mouth. There it leaves the rest of the debris and this sandy material builds up around the mouth, forming sandbars, which over time will change the shape of the coastline.

Why is the mouth of a river sometimes called a "delta?"

The formation of sandbars forces water to find new channels to reach the sea. These channels often cause the mouth of the river to form into the shape of a triangle which resembles the Greek letter, "D" or "delta."

What is an estuary?

Where tidal currents are strong, they do not form sandbars. Instead, they open like a reverse triangle, called an estuary.

Do rivers have "lives?"

Yes. The "childhood" of a river is represented by mountain streams. At this stage, the river flows quickly, falling down over steep hard rocks resistant to erosion. The river moves into "middle age" when it reaches the flatter valleys and plains and flows more slowly, forming wide curves called river bends.

What are cataracts?

These are formed by water falling from one level to another in a short series of steps. Rapids occur when the water flows rapidly down a steep hill.

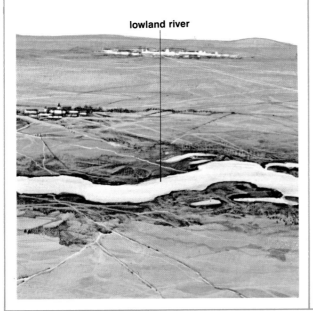
lowland river

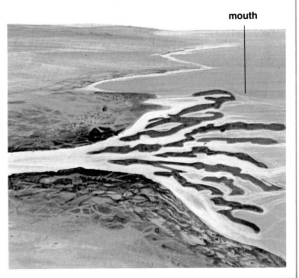
mouth

LAKES

What is a lake?
A lake is a vast expanse of water, usually fresh, contained in a basin-like cavity in the earth's surface and fed by rivers or underground springs.

How are lakes classified?
They are generally classified according to their origin, tectonic, crateric, glacial, etc., what it was that created the concave hole that holds the water.

What are some of the ways in which a lake is formed?
Various natural causes create lakes. Sometimes a lake is formed when the normal flow of a river is blocked. At other times ice, earthquakes, landslides, volcanic eruptions or lava flows make new lakes by creating a basin where the water accumulates naturally.

What are glacial lakes?
They are lakes which fill a cavity carved out by the erosive action of an ancient glacier. A glacier has a very strong erosive force and can cut through the hardest rock, hollowing out a valley until it finally comes to rest. When the glacier eventually melts, it leaves behind one or more basins that fill up with water.

Are there glacier lakes in America?
Yes, there are thousands of small lakes in the northeast, in the upper midwest and in Alaska. The Great Lakes are glacier lakes.

circle lakes

artificial lake

alpine glacial lake

sink-hole lake

lake from glacier deposits

Alpine Lakes

moraine hills

What are tectonic lakes?

They are lakes which occupy a cavity formed by a fracture in the earth's crust. They can be created by an earthquake or by a collapse within the earth's surface. Some of the largest and deepest lakes in the world are tectonic in origin. Two famous ones are Lake Tanganyika in Africa and Lake Baikal in the Soviet Union.

What are crater lakes?

These are lakes which occupy what was once the enclosed crater of a volcano. Volcanic action makes the cavity which then fills up with water.

Are crater lakes always round?

Lakes which occupy the craters of ancient extinguished volcanoes are generally round. Crater Lake in Crater Lake National Park, Oregon, is a famous example.

Do saltwater lakes exist?

Yes, lakes along the seacoast are generally saltwater. These lakes are formed when sand accumulates along the coast and prevents the water from flowing back out to the sea. Saltwater lakes also form when a lake in a very dry region of little rainfall is exposed to massive evaporation. The evaporation leaves behind a large amount of mineral salts. The biggest salt lake in America is the Great Salt Lake in Utah.

Do lakes last forever?

All lakes die eventually, either by drying out or from some other cause. For example, over time the growth of vegetation can transform a shallow lake into a swamp or pond. The erosive action of water causes increasing drainage and the level of the water drops as the lake fills up with mud, rock and other debris. And of course, pollution from all kinds of refuse slowly kills the plants and animals of a lake.

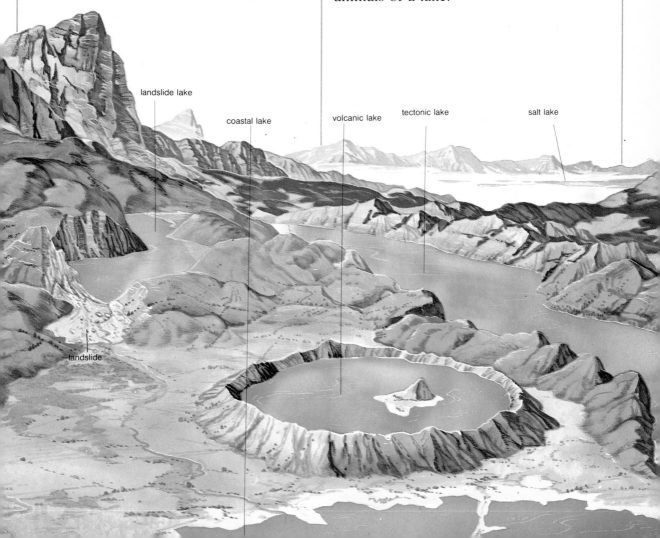

landslide lake

coastal lake

volcanic lake

tectonic lake

salt lake

landslide

PRECIPITATION

Why does water evaporate?
Evaporation is the change of water from a liquid to a gaseous state. This happens when water is heated. Under natural conditions, some water from rivers, lakes, and seas evaporates every day from the heat of the sun's rays.

What is the water cycle?
It is the continuous process of evaporation and precipitation which makes life on earth possible. Water from rivers, lakes and the sea (1, 2, 3) evaporates along with water from the soil (4) and moisture from plant transpiration (giving off leaf water) (5). This moisture comes together in the air to form clouds. Then the water falls back to the earth in condensed form as rain (6), hail and snow (7). The greatest amount of evaporation comes from the oceans' surfaces and the greatest amount of precipitation falls over land. Rivers carry the water from the rain and snow back to the sea and the cycle starts again.

Why are there so many different kinds of clouds?
There are many things that go into making a cloud. The height and temperature at which it forms, the amount of atmospheric pressure and the movement of great currents of air all determine the kind of cloud it becomes. Above you can see two kinds of clouds: cirrocumulus, nicknamed "mares' tails," and cirrus.

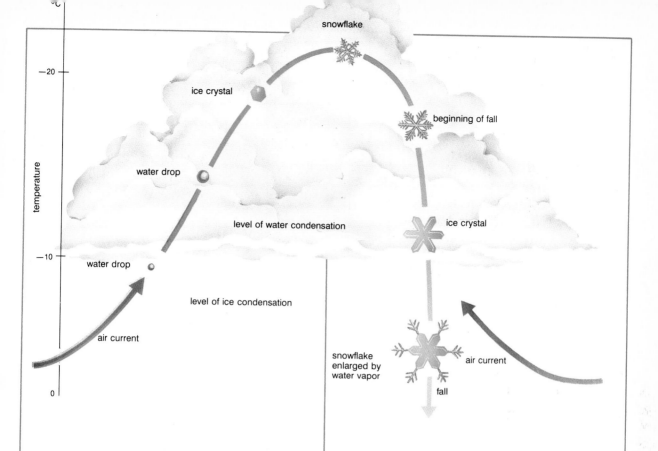

temperature

°C

—20

—10

0

snowflake

ice crystal

water drop

level of water condensation

water drop

level of ice condensation

air current

beginning of fall

ice crystal

snowflake
enlarged by
water vapor

air current

fall

How are clouds formed?

If you heat a kettle of water and keep your eye on the spout where the steam comes out, you will notice that close to the opening the steam is hard to see. But if you look a little way above the spout, you can see the steam better. The steam itself is invisible, but as it expands, it cools and condenses into tiny drops. These drops are what form the clouds that you see above your kettle. In nature they are formed in the same way.

How is rain made?

When tiny drops of water in a cloud fall, they pick up other even tinier drops making them grow larger. As they grow, the drops fall more quickly. The bigger they get, the faster they fall, incorporating more drops. If the cloud is thick enough and the drops get big enough, they fall to earth as rain. Another way that rain is formed is similar to the way snow is formed.

How is snow formed?

A crystal of snow forms inside a cloud. The cloud is formed by the convection or pull of hot humid air rising through colder drier layers in the atmosphere. At the bottom of the cloud, where water condenses, a drop of water is pulled upward on a moving current and eventually it freezes to form a crystal of ice. New molecules of water vapor attach themselves to the crystal creating the rays of a snowflake. The crystal begins to fall, and the rays of the flake grow longer. As the snowflake falls out of the cloud it continues to get bigger. When it falls below the level of condensation of ice, it begins its descent to earth. If the temperature near the ground is above freezing, the ice crystals melt and become rain. But in the winter when temperatures are very low, they reach the ground intact and cover it with a white blanket. Snowflakes have regular geometric forms and look like tiny six-pointed stars.

CAVES

What is speleology?
It is a science that explores and studies caves found under the earth's surface. A speleogist is interested in a part of our planet about which very little was known until the last century.

Are all caves the same?
There are generally two types of caves. One is a "primary" cave which is created during a volcanic eruption. Afterwards, when the lava cools, tunnels form which are sometimes almost four miles long. An example of this kind of cave is the Cuevas de los Verdes located in the Canary Islands. The other kind, a "secondary" cave, is formed in water-permeable limestone after an earthquake, by the erosion of subterranean or surface water penetrating the rock. It has a particularly interesting structure. Some of the most famous caves of this type are in the Carlsbad Caverns National Park in New Mexico and in Mammoth Cave National Park in Kentucky. There also exist small caves in the southwest where people called the Cliff Dwellers lived.

formation of stalactites and stalagmites

two techniques which use double ropes for descending into a cave

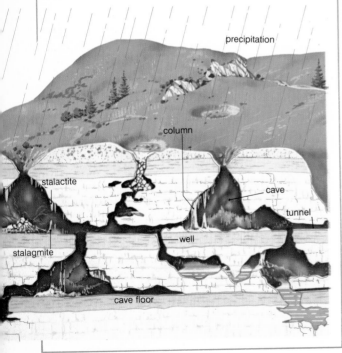

precipitation

column

stalactite

cave

tunnel

well

stalagmite

cave floor

What are the insides of caves like?
They have long passages with holes, some of which are very narrow, connecting them to wide chambers. They can be interrupted by wells, tunnels and special calcium formations such as stalactites and stalagmites.

chimney

What are stalactites and stalagmites?

The water that filters through the roof of a cave is rich in lime carbonate, a mineral. Over the course of centuries, even millenniums, the drops of water, filtering through the cracks in the ceiling, deposit the lime carbonate. Eventually, as the water evaporates, the deposits solidify and form a kind of stone "icicle," a stalactite.

Stalagmites are part of the same phenomenon, except that the mineral solidifies on the ground. Sometimes stalagmites and stalactites grow until they come together and form columns.

Who lives in caves?

Crustaceans, mollusks, insects and certain small animals that have adapted themselves to a damp dark environment live in caves. The strangest of these cave-dwellers is a kind of newt, "Proteus anguinus," that is like a big worm. Completely blind, it is about eight inches long with a whitish, almost transparent "skin," and pink-fringed gills.

Do mammals also live in caves?

There exists only one mammal which lives in the biggest caves, clinging to the walls. It is the bat.

What is the longest cave in the world?

The Mammouth Cave in Kentucky is the longest. It is more than two hundred miles long.

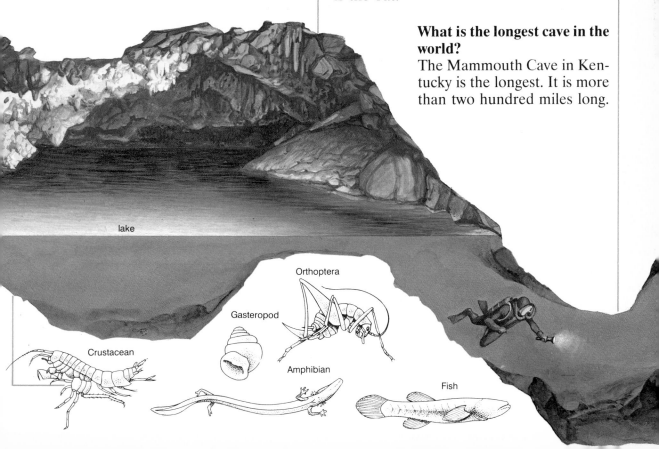

lake

Orthoptera

Gasteropod

Crustacean

Amphibian

Fish

THE DESERT

Have deserts always existed?
No, the vast regions that we call deserts did not always exist. A series of events took place, transforming the landscape and giving it its present appearance. Some deserts are sandy, some of them are covered with a thin layer of rocky soil and some are high mountain mesas cut through by deep gorges. The elements that created all of them are wind, water and the sun.

How do these elements affect the land?
The wind, which will blow very hard if it is not blocked by vegetation, carries with it tiny particles of rock. The rock acts like sandpaper on mountain sides. It crushes, polishes and breaks them into tiny pebbles. Water, in the form of heavy rain, pours down the hills, eroding the softest rocks. Over thousands of years it carves deep gorges out of the rock, carrying sediment to the plains. The sun helps to shatter the hardest rock by exposing it to extreme temperatures.

What are extreme temperatures?
In the daytime the desert floor absorbs ninety per cent of the sun's rays because clouds and atmospheric particles, which weaken the effect of the sun in humid zones, are practically absent. At night, the heat that was so quickly absorbed during the day is completely lost because it is not held in the ground. Therefore, very abrupt changes in temperature occur. It can drop as much as one hundred and four degrees Fahrenheit in a few hours. At night, the temperature in the desert can fall to below freezing. This change in temperature causes rocks to expand and contract constantly, sometimes splitting them open.

rocky soil desert

wadi

Does sand move?

Expanses of sand are not stationary. A windstorm can change the whole landscape, giving the land the characteristic shape of dunes. If the wind is moderate and comes from just one direction, it forms longitudinal ridges. If the wind blows from many directions it forms star-shaped dunes. If the wind is strong and the sand accumulates toward the center of the dune, creating some resistance, only the sand at the edges will scatter, forming crescent-shaped dunes.

Is life possible in the desert?

The difficult climatic conditions have not kept plants and animals from thriving in this environment but they have had to undergo a long period of adaptation. Desert animals work on different "shifts" of activity. Mammals are essentially nocturnal. In order to get food, they must travel long distances which is easier to do during the cool of the night. On the other hand, birds like the little desert wren in the picture, are awake during the day, and nest in the cactus from which they get both water and food. The desert rodent (in the above drawing) goes out both during the day and at night, leaping about with its long stiff tail. It does not perspire and produces very little urine. It can survive for three years without drinking.

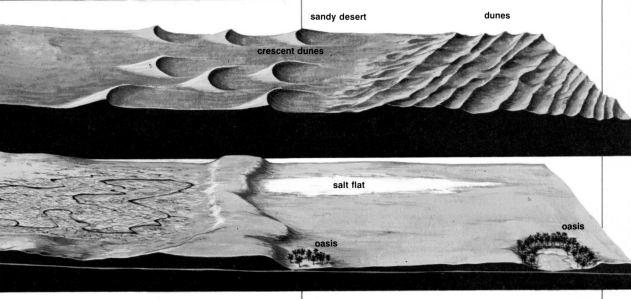

sandy desert

dunes

crescent dunes

salt flat

oasis

oasis

43

THE POLAR REGIONS

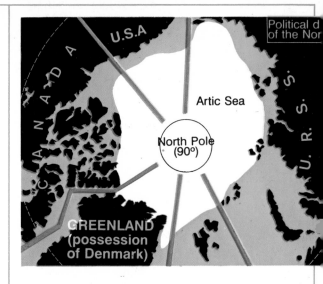

What are the polar regions?
The two ice caps of our planet above the Arctic and Antarctic circles are called polar regions. They are located north of the sixty-sixth parallel.

Do both regions contain land?
While the Antarctic is made up of a vast mountainous region forever covered with ice, the Arctic is a frozen ocean.

Which region is colder?
Because of its tall mountain chain, the Antarctic has registered the coldest temperature on earth, more than one hundred-and-twenty-six degrees below zero!

Why are the poles always frozen?
Because of the tilt of the earth, the sun's rays do not reach the two polar caps perpendicularly, reducing the effect on these regions. Also, because of the earth's rotations, the length of day and night in these regions is much longer compared to our days and nights.

How long is a polar night?
Polar nights can last up to six months at the most extreme point and up to a couple of months around the seventieth parallel.

What are "white nights?"
Because nights can last for entire months in the polar areas, days can, too. You can see what a "white night" is from the series of photographs below. The sun never sets below the horizon and the change from day to night is simply a change in the color of the sky. Deep rose around sunset gradually changes into the softer color of dawn. The farther you get from the poles, the greater the contrast between day and night.

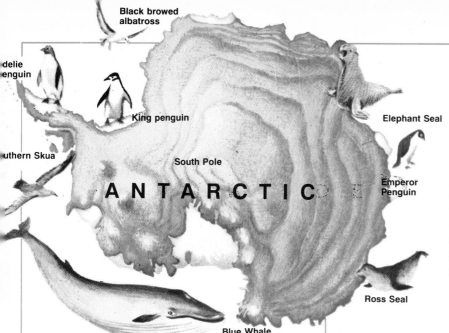

Black browed albatross

Adelie Penguin

King penguin

Southern Skua

South Pole

ANTARCTIC

Elephant Seal

Emperor Penguin

Ross Seal

Blue Whale

To whom do the polar regions belong?

While the Arctic is divided among the countries that border them on the Arctic Sea (see the illustration on the opposite page), the Antarctic, following an international agreement, is considered a zone for scientific research and thus is open to everyone.

Are there seasons as we know them on the poles?

No, it is the absence or presence of the sun which determines the seasons. That is why we talk of a "summer" day and a "winter" night.

What is the aurora borealis?

Also called the "northern lights," it is a phenomenon of light in the atmosphere. It occurs when particles of a rare gas collide with each other. The sky of a polar night will light up in fantastic blue, red, green or yellow lights, depending upon where the collision takes place.

Does anyone live in the polar regions?

In the Arctic region, human settlements can be found as far north as the Svalbard Islands. In the Antarctic, there are some scientific research stations, but many animals live along the coast, such as the penguin, the seal, the elephant seal and the albatross.

What is a tundra?

At the edge of the permafrost region, there is a vast area where, during the long summer days, the snow melts and the land is covered with mosses and lichen. This is the tundra, which during the short summer, is populated with migratory birds, reindeer, foxes, and hares.

DID YOU KNOW...?

What is the average temperature of the earth?
It is seventy-one degrees Fahrenheit on the ground.

Where did the Smoky Mountains get their name?
The Great Smoky Mountains, part of the Appalachians, pass through North Carolina and Tennessee. Their name comes from the smoky haze that is characteristic of the area.

Are there volcanoes on Mars?
Yes. Mars has the biggest volcanoes in the solar system, even though they are now extinguished. The biggest one of all, Mount Olympus, is almost 79,000 feet high.

Which planet has the most satellites?
Saturn. Seventeen satellites have been counted (eight of which were discovered recently).

What are moonquakes?
They are the lunar equivalent of earthquakes.

What is a tributary?
It is water which does not flow directly to the sea but empties into a larger body of water, such as another river.

What are trade winds?
They are winds that blow constantly in tropical zones around the equator. From January to July, they blow toward the north and from July to January, toward the south.

What is a flood?
It is water that overflows its riverbanks after heavy rains.

Where is Mount Ararat?
It is located in Turkey on the border between the Soviet Union and Iran. According to the Bible, it is where Noah landed after the Great Flood.

What is an archipelago?
It is a group of islands lying close together within the same sea.

What is a rainbow?
It is a phenomenon caused by light. It is due to the scattering and bending of sunlight as it passes through raindrops. You can see it in the sky during a rainstorm. It forms an arch and contains all the colors of the spectrum from red to violet.

Who was the first cosmonaut?
He was Yuri Gagarin, who on April 12th, 1961, carried out the first space orbit around the earth on board the Russian spacecraft, Vostok I.

What does atmosphere mean?
The atmosphere is the envelope of gas that surrounds some stars and planets. The earth's atmosphere extends more than 62,000 miles above our planet.

What is an anti-cyclone?
It is a high-pressure area and the opposite of a cyclone, which is a low-pressure area. Anti-cyclones often cause undisturbed stable weather.

What is a canyon?
"Cañon" in Spanish means "canal." It refers to a deep narrow valley which is created by the flow of water over thousands of years. The Grand Canyon is a very famous canyon.

Why is the sky blue in the daytime?
The blue color of the sky is an optical illusion. It looks blue to us because the white light of the sun spreads the blue rays with greater intensity.

What are cirrus clouds?
They are very high clouds, between 19,000 and 32,000 feet, formed by tiny needles of ice. They are characterized by their transparency and by their long strip-like shape. Cirrus clouds signal bad weather.

PEOPLE AND
CIVILIZATIONS

THE FIRST PEOPLE

Are humans really descendants of apes?

The most recent research says no. Instead, humans and apes may be "cousins," descended from a common ancestor, Driopithecus, who lived between twenty and ten million years ago. This creature lived in the forests and survived by eating plants. He was between two and four feet tall.

Was Australopithecus a human?

No, but Australopithecus, who lived between three and one million years ago, had many human characteristics, especially those linked to behavior and organization of daily life. He ate plants as well as meat obtained by hunting.

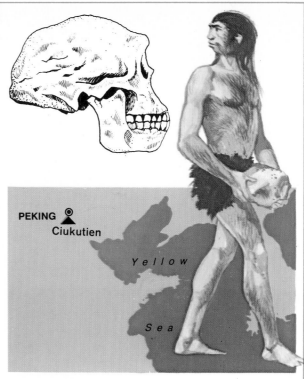

Who was Peking man?

He was one of our more recent ancestors. He lived half a million years ago. He is so named because his remains were found in a cave near a village about fifty miles from Peking.

When were his remains found?

The first important remains were found in December 1929. But a few years earlier, scientists had discovered two teeth there. This made them wonder about the possibility of a new species of humans and gave them the idea that the cave might hold other remains as well.

Was only one fossil found?

No. The cave held the fossil remains of some forty humans of the "Homo erectus" species, which is the same as the Peking man but from a different era, some as recent as 200,000 years ago. The cave also contained the first reliable proof that early people knew how to make and use fire.

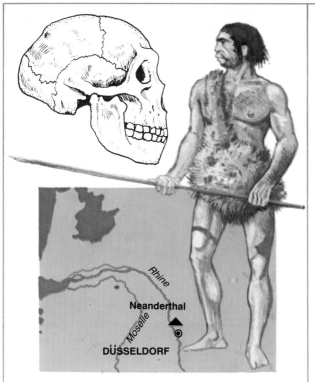

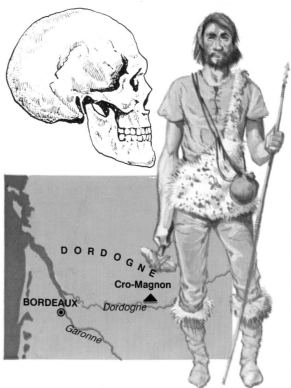

Who was Neanderthal man?
He was one of the first representatives of the species, "Homo sapiens," to which we belong. We do not know how people evolved from "Homo erectus" to "Homo sapiens," but the Neanderthals are the oldest examples of this new species, living from 100,000 to 60,000 years ago. The first remains of a Neanderthal were found in 1856, but their age and importance were not recognized until much later, in the 1950s.
Neanderthal man had a thickset body and short arms and legs. He used simple tools to shape awls and blades. He buried his dead in tombs and had complicated funeral rites, accompanied by offerings to the gods.

How did Neanderthal get his name?
The first fossil remains were discovered in a cave near Dusseldorf in a little valley in northern Germany, along the river Neander, a tributary of the Rhine River. "Thal" means valley in German.

Who was Cro-Magnon man?
The Neanderthals were one of two sub-species of "Homo sapiens." The other sub-species was "Homo sapiens sapiens," our species. Cro-Magnon man was one of its oldest representatives, appearing around 35,000 years ago. A skull and skeleton of Cro-Magnon man were found in 1868 in the Dordogne, France, together with many stone tools and various animal bones from the same period. Art was born during that period in the form of wall-paintings.
Cro-Magnon, the name of this area, has been given to species of humans very similar to us, who lived between 60,000 and 10,000 years ago.

Are there traces of Cro-Magnon man in other places?
Yes. Sixteen skeletons of Cro-Magnon man were discovered in Liguria, Italy, in the caves of Balzi Rossi. Almost two hundred skeletons of primitive people which can be classified as Cro-Magnon have been discovered around the world.

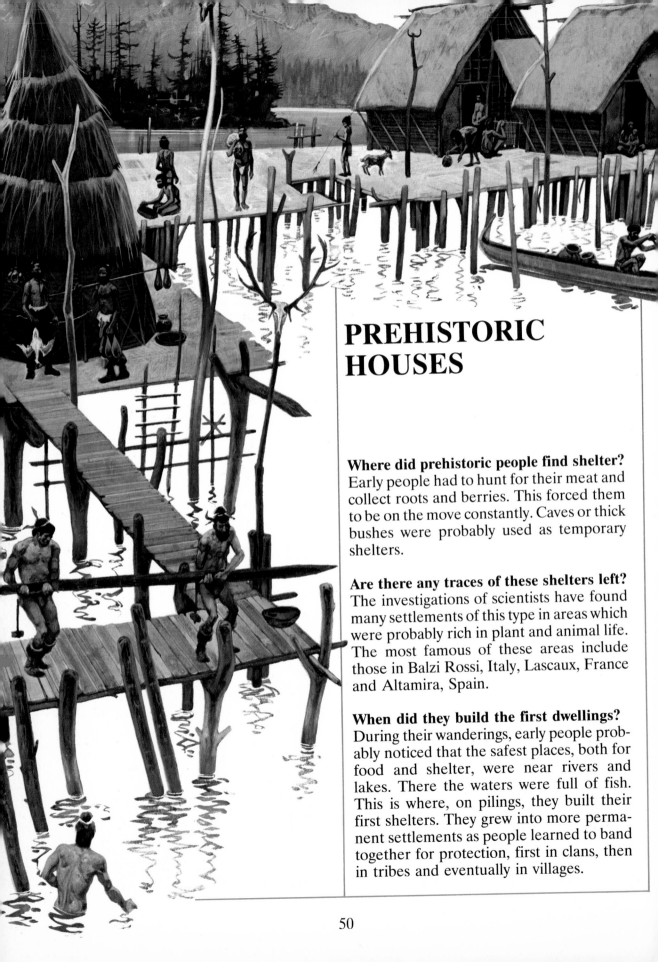

PREHISTORIC HOUSES

Where did prehistoric people find shelter?
Early people had to hunt for their meat and collect roots and berries. This forced them to be on the move constantly. Caves or thick bushes were probably used as temporary shelters.

Are there any traces of these shelters left?
The investigations of scientists have found many settlements of this type in areas which were probably rich in plant and animal life. The most famous of these areas include those in Balzi Rossi, Italy, Lascaux, France and Altamira, Spain.

When did they build the first dwellings?
During their wanderings, early people probably noticed that the safest places, both for food and shelter, were near rivers and lakes. There the waters were full of fish. This is where, on pilings, they built their first shelters. They grew into more permanent settlements as people learned to band together for protection, first in clans, then in tribes and eventually in villages.

HOW SHELTERS DEVELOPED

First, they made a simple lean-to out of sticks.

They put a hole in the center for a fire.
Outside, mud was caked on for reinforcement.

The shelter is then buried with a roof covering a hole in the ground.

Walls then appear and emerge from the ground.

The shelter now looks like a real house.

How were these first houses built?

Early people used branches, tree trunks and straw as building materials. The first structures were tent-like and rested on wooden pilings, supported by long poles sunk into the water.

Why were they built in the water?

Such dwellings, connected to land by planks that could be pulled up when night fell, offered people safe shelter from rain and cold, ferocious animals and even attacks from other tribes. Dwellings like these have been found throughout the European Alps, where there are many lakes. In the "New World," important Indian lake dwelling sites still exist in South America.

When were the first permanent villages built?

People only settled in more permanent communities when they began to grow crops. This gave them a constant and reliable source of food, allowing them to stay in one place. The first permanent dwellings were built of stone, brick and clay over ten thousand years ago.

What were the first houses like?

With the discovery of a prehistoric village on the island of Cyprus, we can reconstruct the structure of the first houses. They were circular with a domed roof. Inside, in the center was the hearth and around the walls existed built-in platforms where people slept. There was also a storage area above the ground floor where they could keep food.

What is the oldest city?

We now think the oldest city was Jericho in Palestine. From excavations, we can guess that the city was surrounded by strong walls which protected the houses that were inside. The people worked on land outside the city walls.

SCIENCE IN ANCIENT TIMES

What did people in ancient times think about the earth?

The Babylonians believed that the earth was round but flat. Over four thousand years ago, they drew a picture of the earth on a clay tablet (see illustration at right). Mountains are represented by circles and the rivers by parallel lines. In the center is Babylon.

429 + 253 = 682

What was the first "calculator?"

It was the abacus (above), used by the Babylonians. It was a tablet with three columns carved in it which contained small pebbles. The first column on the right was for units, the center for tens and the last for hundreds.

What could you do with it?

One could add as well as subtract by using the abacus. You only had to add or remove the pebbles corresponding to units, tens and hundreds, just like we do today when we add up columns of numbers to carry out such operations. When the units went beyond ten, you removed them and added them to the tens column.

Did the Babylonians study science?

Yes, they were interested in astronomy and carried out observations of the skies. Five thousand years ago, Babylonian priests could predict eclipses of the sun (pictured at right). Because they were able to keep notes of their observations, they became able mathematicians.

What were the results of their observations?

They were able to calculate the dates of the solstices and the equinoxes, the courses of the planets and the orbits of the sun and moon. They also developed a very precise calendar, dividing the year into twelve lunar months and each month into four weeks. This division however, only gave them three-hundred-and-fifty-four days in a year which does not coincide exactly with the phases of the moon. Because of this, occasionally they added a thirteenth month.

Were there other systems used by ancient man for counting and measuring time?

Among the Incas, elaborate cords with knots were used (see the illustration a-bove). The color indicated the kind of object to be counted (animals, gold, days) and the knots, the quantity.

The Aztecs calculated the year by using a round stone calendar (illustrated below).

THE PHARAOHS

How many pharaoh dynasties existed?
As best we know, there were thirty one dynasties. They covered a period in history from around the year 3,100 B.C., when Egypt was unified into a single kingdom, to the year 332 B.C., when Alexander the Great conquered Egypt.

Who unified Egypt?
Around 3,100 B.C., Narmer, the priest-king of Thinis, a city in Upper Egypt, conquered the whole Nile Valley up to the delta. Narmer, who unified Egypt, was the first pharaoh and he founded the first dynasty. He was considered to be the son of the falcon-god, Horus, the ancient symbol of the sun. The pharaohs of the first dynasty were warrior-kings, conquering Nubia, which we now call the Sudan. Their political conquests were accompanied by important developments in crafts and trade in raw materials, because of their contacts with the people of Mesopotamia. In the illustration below, the pharaoh, standing in his reviewing cart, inspects military troops in Nubia.

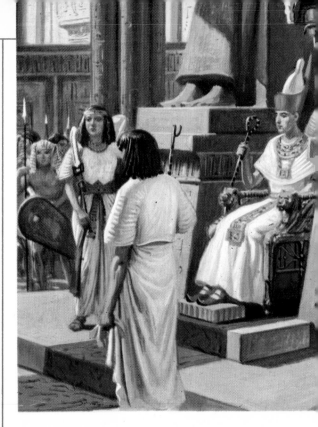

Who was the "vizier?"
He was in charge of administration and second in command after the pharaoh. He took care of the governing of the city and all of Egypt.

When were the pyramids built?

The pyramid was the characteristic shape of the tombs of the pharaohs of the Ancient and Middle Kingdoms. These historical periods went from the third to the thirteenth dynasty. The oldest example of a pyramid was in Saqqara. It was a stepped pyramid built by Zoser, a pharaoh of the third dynasty, around 2,660 B.C. The typical form of the pyramids was adopted during the fourth dynasty. It reached its high point in terms of size and complexity, in the pyramid of Cheops. According to Heredotus, its construction took thirty years and 1,000,000 slaves. After the fourth dynasty, the pharaohs began to build smaller pyramids: they too, had problems with the high cost of labor and building materials.

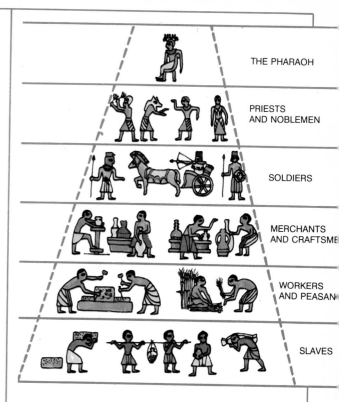

THE PHARAOH

PRIESTS AND NOBLEMEN

SOLDIERS

MERCHANTS AND CRAFTSME

WORKERS AND PEASAN

SLAVES

How was Egyptian society organized?

The social structure of ancient Egypt was another kind of pyramid. At the top was the pharaoh. Just below him, next to the vizier and the nobility, were the priests. The task of the priests was to keep the gods happy through prayers and sacrifices and to interpret their wishes. They also took care of the "houses of life," attached to the temples where reading and writing were taught. A select few went on to study the subjects revealed by the gods: mathematics, geometry, medicine, the techniques of administration and arts and letters. Below this rank were the soldiers who also enjoyed great prestige. On the bottom half of the pyramid were the workers. Egypt was basically an enormous agricultural farm made fertile by the regular flooding of the Nile. In fact, the greater part of Egyptian paintings and carvings shows people at work in the fields. Most peasants were free citizens. Slaves were assigned to domestic work or work in mining, alongside condemned criminals. Women were given tasks requiring the most education.

THE ORIGINS OF WRITING

Did the Sumerians invent writing?

We cannot say for certain although it is true that the oldest clay tablets found contain incisions that are certainly Sumerian. These tablets date back to around 3,500 B.C. They were found in excavations of the ancient Sumerian cities of Uruk and Kish. They are records of the movement of merchandise from warehouses, leading us to believe that perhaps writing was invented to meet administrative needs. The marks on the tablets are actually drawings. That is why this writing is called pictographic.

Who first deciphered hieroglyphics?

Below you can see the two words that allowed the French archeologist, Champollion, to decipher Egyptian hieroglyphic writing. He did this by comparing the two texts, hieroglyphics and Greek, side by side. He found them on the Rosetta Stone, a slab of black basalt, discovered by a scientific mission which accompanied Napoleon to Egypt. From the Greek text, Champollion figured out that the inscription was dedicated to the king, Ptolomy. Where one would imagine the name of the king to be, he found a group of drawings enclosed in an oval ring called a "cartouche." Arranging the letters of the name "Ptolomy" under the drawings of the cartouche, he discovered which letters of the alphabet corresponded to which drawing. Then he did the same with "Cleopatra".

Cleopatra   Ptolomy

Did the Hittites write on metal?

Yes, but rolls of lead like the one pictured below were not the most common means of written communication. Generally, the Hittites wrote with a pen and ink on wood tablets which were then covered with linen and whitewashed.

Were Egyptian hieroglyphics pictographs?

No, most of them were ideograms and some had phonetic value. They represented certain consonant sounds (vowels were not represented). Pictographs represent the object drawn while ideograms indicate not only the objects themselves but also other similar objects or ideas. In Sumerian writing some pictographs were already being replaced by ideograms. Once the Sumerians began to change their writing, it evolved rapidly, becoming increasingly more stylized, until it turned into syllabic writing, where the symbols represented syllables. This eventually developed into cuneiform (wedge-shaped) writing because it was easier to trace pointed lines in soft clay using sticks with triangular tips.

Are Chinese characters ideograms?

For the most part they are. Each word of the language is written with characters that can be reduced to a certain number of figures. These figures are images or symbols. The first represents a thing, a tree, for example, and the second an idea or an action for instance, to eat. There used to be tens of thousands of Chinese characters and even today there are some three to five thousand characters still in common use.

Who invented the alphabet?

Most scholars believe that the alphabet was invented by the Phoenicians. They date it from around 1,500 B.C. The Greeks learned it from the Phoenicians and they taught it to the Etruscans who gave it to the Romans. The Latin alphabet, created by the Romans, is the one we use today.

Phoenician,

𐤀 9 1 ⅄ ⅁ ⅄ Y I H Θ ⅂ Ч L ⅄ Y ‡ O Ↄ Γ Q ⅁ w X

Greek

ΑΒΓΔΕΥZΗΘΙΚΛΜΝΞΟΠΨ ΡΣΤ

Latin

ABCDEVZH IKLMN OP QRST

THE GREEKS

When was the birth of Greek civilization?
The early centuries of Greek civilization are somewhat confusing. The only written testimony for that period comes from the myths and legends collected by such poets as Hesiod and Homer. Homer wrote the *Iliad*, a narrative poem that describes the long war which the Greeks waged against the city of Troy. It is rich in detail about the lives and customs of those days. The poem describes an aristocratic society in which power was in the hands of a few princes and noble warriors.

Were the poems that Homer wrote legends?
Modern archeology, starting with the discovery of the remains of ancient Troy by the German, Heinrich Schliemann, in the last century, proved that Homer's poems contained not only fantastic imagery but also many elements of truth. This was confirmed by later discoveries, such as the remains of the ancient cities of Pylos, Tirinth and Mycenae, including noble houses surrounded by huge stone walls and grand tombs full of precious pottery and gold.

What was a Greek city like?
Each city, called a "polis," was an autonomous political, cultural and commercial center. It was surrounded by a wall and contained an acropolis, a raised area were the temples of the most important gods were located. The acropolis was used as the last point of defense. Each city also had a town square, the "agora," for its commercial activity and for assemblies of the people.
In the illustration below you can see the acropolis of Athens, the biggest and richest of the Greek cities.

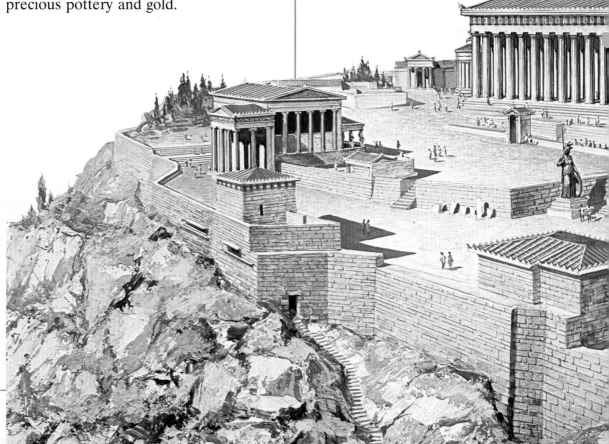

Which were the most important Greek cities?

There were many city states in Greece. Corinth was a commercial city, and Delphi and Thebes were two other important cities. The most important cities were Athens and Sparta, each different in its own way and each hostile to the other. Athens was a democracy, the home of artists and philosophers. Sparta was governed by an aristocracy and its citizen warriors were always working to maintain and build up its powerful army.

Did Athens and Sparta ever go to war?

The Greek cities were often at war. Athens and Sparta were involved in a conflict that lasted more than thirty years, called the Peloponnesian war, which ended in the short-lived victory of Sparta.

Why was it short-lived?

Because after a period of peace, the freedom of the "poleis" was swept away with the arrival of the Macedonians. Led by Philip II of Macedonia, the father of the famous Alexander the Great, the Macedonian forces defeated the Greeks at Chaeronea, creating a vast empire. This showed the importance of a military strategy. The Macedonian army was a powerful one and the military backwardness of the Greeks was revealed when the Greeks faced the sharp points of the Macedonians' lances.

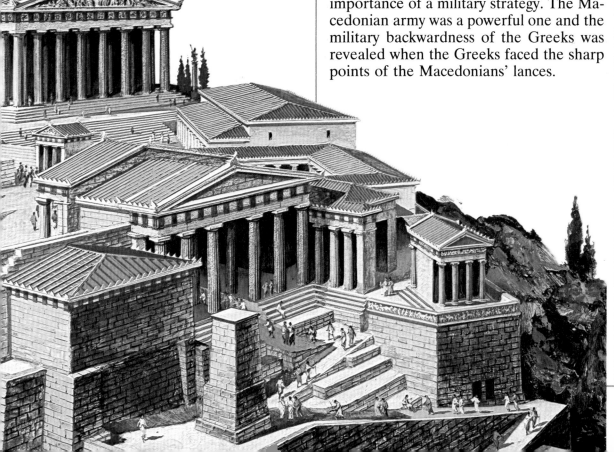

ROMAN HOUSES

What kind of houses did the ancient Romans have?

Because the Romans were excellent architects, they knew how to find practical and original solutions for their houses. The kind of house a person lived in, however, depended a great deal on his economic and social class. The "domus" drawn below, was meant for the privileged classes, while ordinary citizens lived in "insulae," small houses on different floors similar to our modern apartment buildings.

What kind of objects were found in these houses?

In the photo below you can see the hearth of a house in Pompeii containing some pots, a grater and, in the foreground, a loaf of charred bread. This was not as comfortable as a house in Rome where you would find elegantly decorated silver amphora, cups and glasses displayed. Roman houses were lit with clay, bronze or silver oil-burning lamps which were suspended from the ceiling or from special hooks.

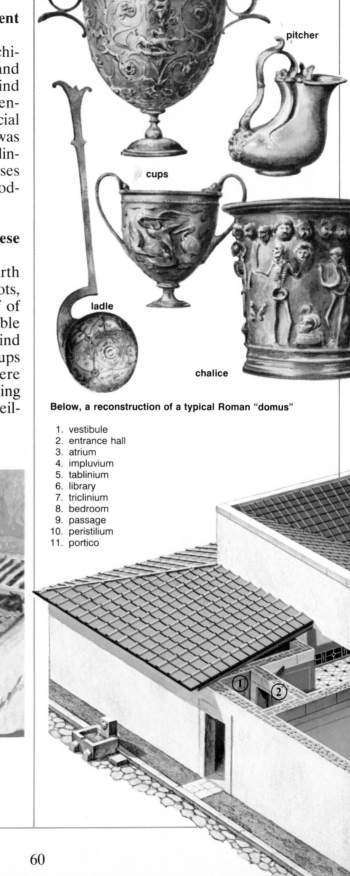

pitcher

cups

ladle

chalice

Below, a reconstruction of a typical Roman "domus"

1. vestibule
2. entrance hall
3. atrium
4. impluvium
5. tablinium
6. library
7. triclinium
8. bedroom
9. passage
10. peristilium
11. portico

What was a "domus" like?

The drawing below clearly shows the interior of a wealthy person's house. Part of the roof has been removed so you can better see the arrangement and furnishings of the rooms. Just beyond the entrance there is a large atrium, the compluvium, that is partially exposed to let in the light. Below it is a rectangular basin, the impluvium, to collect rain water. Around the atrium, there are several rooms used for different purposes. There is a dining room, the triclinium, a bedroom, and some smaller rooms occupied by the servants or used as storerooms for household belongings. At the back of the atrium is the tablinium, a room for study or meetings facing the interior garden or peristilium. The garden was usually carefully attended and decorated with fountains and statues. Around it there is a covered passageway leading to other rooms. The Roman house was built of stone or brick and was usually one story high.

How was the house furnished?

The furnishings also changed according to the wealth of the owner. Generally, the walls of Roman houses were bare and the rooms only lightly furnished. Most objects were placed in storerooms and the public rooms contained only certain indispensable items like beds, tables and stools. Sometimes however, in the homes of the rich, the walls of the most important rooms were decorated with elegant and refined frescoes or wall painting (you can still admire them today at the Villa dei Misteri in Pompeii). Furniture was made of highly prized materials such as rare woods, marble, bronze, ivory, tortoiseshell and silver. The "insulae" contained few pieces of furniture that were made of more humble materials.

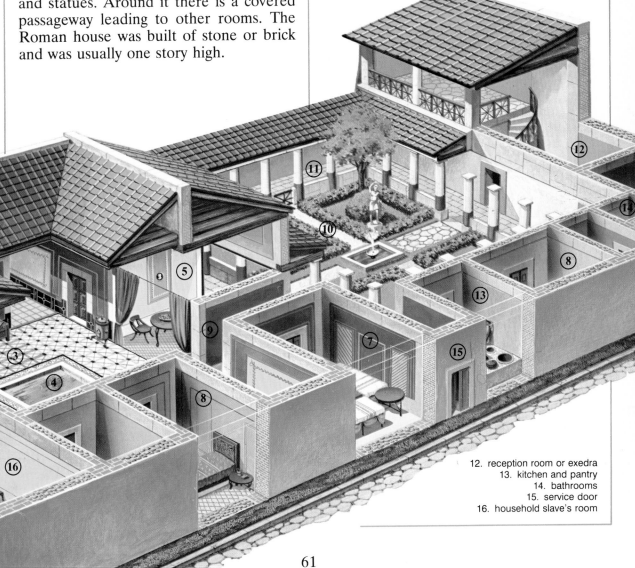

12. reception room or exedra
13. kitchen and pantry
14. bathrooms
15. service door
16. household slave's room

ROMAN ENTERTAINMENT

Did the Romans go to the theater?

Theater, which came from the Greeks, was common among the Romans, too. Comedy was the most successful kind of theater production in Rome. Plays were written by such great writers as Plautus and Terence, who took their ideas from the Greek playwrights. Nevertheless, the theater was considered rather vulgar, good only for servants, freedmen and foreigners. Roman citizens were much more attracted to violent spectacles, such as gladiator fights and chariot races.

Who were the gladiators?

Gladiators were generally prisoners who were forced to become slaves or freedmen who fought ferocious beasts or other gladiators. Before beginning combat the "athletes" kneeled before the box of the emperor and greeted him saying, "Ave Caesar, the dying greet you."

When Caesar gave the order to begin combat, the gladiators, in pairs, competed in fierce battle. If one of the two contenders lost his weapon, he had to wait for the public and the emperor to decide if he should be saved or not. This was expressed with the thumb: "thumbs up" meant life, "thumbs down" meant death. There were other variations of this spectacle, such as gladiators fighting on horseback, in battle-carts, in groups or against wild beasts.

How could you tell one gladiator from another?

Although the word "gladiator" comes from "gladius," a Latin word for a short sword with a wide blade, used by the Roman legionnaires, not all gladiators were armed in the same way. They were divided into groups depending upon what weapon they used. The names included, "thracius," "retiarrius," "secutors," and "mirmillo," also called Gauls.

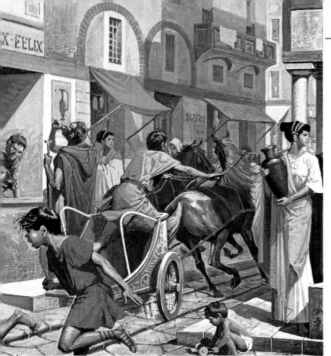

Where did the gladiators fight?

They fought in arenas or amphitheaters with oval-shaped fields. In the largest ones, complicated mechanisms partially flooded the field so naval battles could be fought.

What was the Roman circus?

The circus was a building which had a rectangular field with rounded ends. Chariot racing, a very popular form of entertainment, was held there. The chariots were light carts pulled by two horses which could carry a driver and a passenger. Once upon a time they were used in wars. A variation of the chariot, or "biga," was the "quadriga," drawn by four horses. To get an idea of how popular this sport was, the winner could win from one to sixty thousand sesterce, which was a great deal of money in those days.

What kind of weapons did gladiators use?

The "thracius" used a curved dagger and a round shield. The "retiarius" used a net and a trident. The "secutor" was a pursuer and used a large shield and a short sword. The "mirmillo" had a heavy helmet, a small shield and a long sword.

Were there other public gathering places?

In the Imperial Age, public baths, besides being places to take a hot or cold bath, had other rooms for resting, reading, and holding meetings. Some even had libraries. They were also places where men and women could meet their friends.

MARCO POLO

When did the great voyages of exploration begin?
They began in the thirteenth century, when the population was growing and cities all over Europe were getting bigger. Travel between cities grew easier allowing more goods to be traded. This created a new merchant class whose members were able to accumulate enormous wealth in a short time. This allowed them to buy fleets of ships and travel to far-off countries that until then had been heard of only in stories.

Were the expeditions successful?
Many attempts, like that of the Vivaldi brothers, failed. They left Genoa in 1291 with two ships, the *Allegranza* and the *Saint Antonio* (illustrated far left), and traveled along the coast of Africa, hoping to find another route to India. That way they hoped to get products from India directly, without having to go through intermediaries. Unfortunately, they were never heard of again.

Who was the first to sail around Africa successfully?
A Portuguese explorer, Vasco da Gama, was the first to sail this route succesfully two centuries after the courageous attempt by the Vivaldi brothers.

Why were merchants trying to reach India?
Because India was where the spices were grown that the Europeans treasured so highly. At that time India was the name Europeans used for all of the Far East. They knew about it from Arab merchants who had established links between Asia and Europe and sold the Europeans their spices. Then the European merchants wanted to buy directly from Asia. The first expeditions left from port cities in Europe, especially Genoa and Venice in Italy.

Who were the Polos?
They were a Venetian merchant family who crossed Asia overland to reach the Far East, following the efforts of Giovanni da Pian del Carpine, a Franciscan who had traveled on foot from Umbria in Italy to Mongolia. In a second voyage, Niccolo Polo took his seventeen-year-old son, Marco, with him.

What route did they take?
The Polos traveled by sea from Venice to Acre. From there they headed north through the Arab countries, and crossing the Himalayas, they finally reached Beijing.

How was young Marco received in the East?
The Great Khan became a good friend of Marco. He soon accepted him as one of his counselors and entrusted him with many commissions. This allowed the young man to spend almost twenty years in the Khan's splendid court and to become familiar with the customs and habits of the fabulous East. His stories, when he returned home, astonished the Venetians.

Who wrote of Marco Polo's adventures?
A fellow prisoner wrote of these adventures. For Marco, upon his return to Venice, was taken prisoner by the Genoans after a battle between the them and the Venetians.

What is the book called?
In English it is called *The Travels of Marco Polo*. In Italian, however, it was called *Millions* because when Marco spoke of China, he was always saying, ". . .millions of people, millions of riches, millions of soldiers."

THE FIRST BOOK

Who printed the first book?

A German craftsman named Johannes Gutenberg printed the first book. He designed a system around the middle of the fifteenth century that allowed him to print the first book, the Bible. Books became very important because they made it easier to spread the written word.

How did Gutenberg print his book?

The system he invented used "movable type." This method continued to be used until very recently, when technology revolutionized printing.

What is "movable type?"

It is a kind of stamp, called a punch, on which is engraved a letter of the alphabet. Punches can be arranged to form a word (see illustration at right).

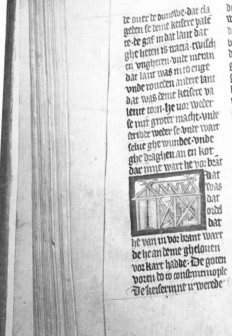

abcdefghi ABCDE

How were things printed before Gutenberg's invention?

Before Gutenberg, books were handwritten and illustrated with miniature paintings. For centuries the same methods were used to reproduce images. All kinds of figures were engraved on a special kind of wooden stamp. The stamp, dipped in a color, was then pressed down onto paper and the image reproduced. Similar attempts were made using letters of the alphabet, but it was a complicated procedure because of the small size of the engraving and because the wood was easily damaged.

What did Gutenberg do?

As the wooden stamps did not work well, he decided to carve a full-page mold out of clay. Over this he poured a mixture of melted lead and tin. When it cooled, he broke the clay away from the metal. He was left with a whole page in metal with the characters in relief (standing out). Onto this, he spread his ink and in this way was able to print a whole page at a time. Of course, after he finished printing the page, it was useless, so he had to start over again each time. Then the idea occurred to him to use the same process but with individual movable letters. That way he could use them again later to print other texts.

Why was his invention so important?

Gutenberg's system made it possible to reproduce texts that until then had always been written by hand. Before his invention, there were only a few copies of each book and only a few people were able to read them. After Gutenberg, the number of books printed was exceptional. As many as two thousand copies of a single book could be made. Gutenberg's idea was improved upon over time. For example, the style of type evolved (for an example of Gothic script, see the illustration, far left). As the years passed, the shape of letters was simplified until they came to look as they do today.

What is linotype?

At the end of the last century, machines were invented that could cast and coin different letters of the alphabet. This machine, the linotype, could be used like an ordinary typewriter, creating words and arranging them in lines that would be joined together to make a page.

line of type from a linotype machine

THE RENAISSANCE

What was the Renaissance?

This word indicates a cultural phenomenon that affected all of human activity. It profoundly changed the social and political structures of the time and the way man thought about existence, art and literature. In fact it affected his whole way of living. This change was called the Renaissance or "rebirth" because it emphasized new ideas as opposed to the old ones of the Middle Ages. The old ideas had tried to suppress the cultural evolution of man.

When and where did it happen?

The Renaissance began in Italy around 1400 A.D., and lasted until the end of the sixteenth century. It spread all over Europe from Italy creating new interest in art and scholarship.

What caused it to develop?

The Renaissance grew out of the courts of the great families of Italy. These wealthy men and women liked to surround themselves with artists and men of culture whose presence brought prestige to the nobles. The lords in turn protected the artists and became their benefactors. The luxurious palaces of the lords and the castles of the powerful became true centers of culture where men studied, worked and created beautiful things. The artists used all their efforts to please and honor their patrons and the works of painting, sculpture, architecture and literature left by them are incomparable. Around these courts, other centers of culture developed, like academies where artists and writers could meet. The first libraries, also supported by the great lords, were constructed then, too. Pictured below you can see the city of Florence, Italy as it might have looked in those days.

What characterized the Renaissance?

Above all, the Renaissance was a rediscovery of ancient civilizations, especially those of the Greeks and the Romans. They were studied through the creation of a new science, philology, the study of language. Another characteristic was the reevaluation of man as a thinking being. Renaissance men believed that a man's destiny did not depend only on religion or the will of a god, but was also a product of his actions and his choices. A new understanding of nature developed, producing a mine of knowledge unknown before, bringing with it great progress in both medicine and physics. The arts and literature were considered the greatest achievements of the creative capacity of man and were considered to be the best way to gain immortality.

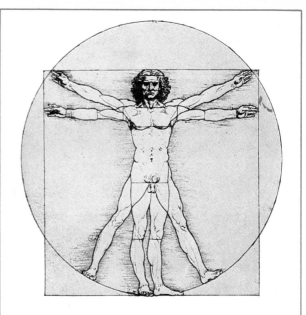

What innovations were created in the fields of science and technology during this period?

Renaissance culture produced many important discoveries in geography, science and technology. Man, filled with a desire to know and see new things, invented better instruments of navigation and ventured out over the seas in great ships. In 1488 A.D., Diaz was the first to reach the tip of Africa. In 1497 A.D., Vasco da Gama reached India. In 1519 A.D., Magellan circumnavigated (sailed completely around) the earth. But the most important discovery was that of America in 1492 A.D. by Christopher Columbus.

Also important, because of the extraordinary consequences it had, was Gutenberg's discovery of movable type in 1457 A.D., which allowed him to print the first book, the Bible. Other inventions worth mentioning were firearms and gunpowder, which completely changed the way people fought wars. In the natural sciences, the curative (curing) properties of plants were studied, leading to the development of the modern science, botany. The human body was also studied, and this science, called anatomy, led to important changes in medicine and, a little later, to the foundation of the modern sciences. Above, you can see an anatomy study drawn by Leonardo da Vinci.

PIRATES

What were pirates?
Pirates were robbers of the high seas who attacked ships, plundering and stealing their goods.

When did they first appear?
Piracy was practised from early times in the Mediterranean. The Phoenicians were good sailors and often bold pirates. During the Middle Ages, it was sometimes hard to distinguish between battles of conquest, as with the Normans and the Arabs, and pirate attacks. By the nineteenth century piracy had almost disappeared except in some places around Indonesia. One unusual case in pirate history was that of the Barbary Coast, a true pirate state set up in North Africa beginning in the sixteenth century. Until the end of the nineteenth century, it was dangerous to sail in the Mediterranean.

Who were the pirates of the Atlantic Ocean?
After the discovery of America, trade between the New World and Europe became very important. Ships leaving the colonies were filled with all kinds of goods. These riches attracted many English, Dutch and French adventurers and there were even pirate groups along the British coast which were controlled by English noblemen.

Who were the freebooters?
The freebooters were a kind of pirate who, between the seventeenth and eighteenth centuries, conducted a ruthless war against the Spanish in the Antilles. They captured and plundered galleons and invaded the coastal outposts of the colonies. The French from Tortuga, the English from Jamaica and the Dutch from the Dutch Antilles often sailed together as allies with the buccaneers.

Did pirates live by any rules?
Yes. Their duties were regulated by written rules which established an iron-clad discipline to be followed aboard. An infraction, such as smoking in the hold, was punishable according to Moses' Law, "forty stripes mi-

nus one on the bare back." If a pirate was wounded in battle he received a larger share of the booty (stolen goods).

Who were the buccaneers?
Originally, they were colonists who raised oxen in the Antilles and sold the hides and meat, which they cured in special smokehouses called "boucans." Expelled from the Bahamas by the English in 1629 and from

San Cristoforo in 1630 by the Spanish, the buccaneers joined the privateers in Tortuga. One of the most famous was Sir Henry Morgan, who raided Panama, Spain's richest town in the New World, in 1671, probably under orders from the English. There were also female pirates in that century. Two of the most famous were Anne Bonny and Mary Reed.

Who were the corsairs?
Corsairs, or privateers, were part of the crew of private ships commissioned by governments to try to break the Spanish trade monopoly in the Antilles. They were authorized by their sovereigns under a letter of marque to attack and loot enemy ships. Their task was to conduct acts of war to weaken the enemy forces. In the Antilles, this was directed mainly against the Spanish.

Who were the most famous corsairs?
Francis Drake, who played a prominent role in the creation of the English colonial empire, and Captain Kidd were two of the most famous corsairs.

What kinds of weapons and ships did the pirates use?
They used pistols, cutlasses, boarding axes, daggers and blunderbusses as personal weapons. For ships, they wanted strong, fast boats. Some of the ones they used were the schooner, small and fast with two masts, the sloop, with a single mast and square topsail, the square rigger, with twenty cannons, and the brigantine, a fast, sturdy two-masted ship. Boats with large caliber cannons fired a pair of cannon balls attached to chains to break the masts of vessels.

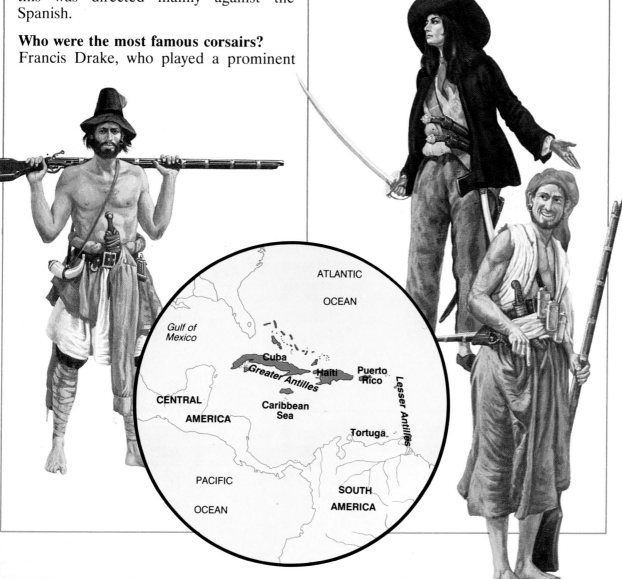

THE FRENCH REVOLUTION

When did the French Revolution occur?
The exact date, which changed the fate not only of France but of the whole world, was July 14, 1789. That was the day Parisians attacked the Bastille, the jail where political prisoners were held. But, as with all historic events, this was the result of a long series of events over several years that continued even after 1789.

Who was governing France at the time?
As in most of Europe, France was governed by an absolute monarch, King Louis XVI. This meant that the laws governing the country were established by him and his attendants who belonged to the nobility and the church. The third estate was excluded completely.

What was the "third estate?"
It was a new social class, formed in the Middle Ages. It was made up of people who did not live on the income of their lands as did the nobles, or the wealth of the church, as did the clergy. These people, who were craftsmen and merchants, lived on the money that they earned themselves. Following the Industrial Revolution in the eighteenth century in England, the means of production changed completely and there were more people earning money. As their numbers grew, they wanted to have more say in the running of the country to protect their own interests.

What was decided with the "Tennis Court Oath?"
In June, 1789, representatives of the third estate met secretly to decide to put an end to the power of the nobles and the church, swearing to carry out their task to the end. The meeting was held in a place where a kind of lawn tennis, an ancestor of modern tennis, was played.

72

Why did the third estate have the support of the people?

Peasants and workers lived in miserable conditions, and were forced to pay high taxes to support the aristocracy. Injustice was the order of the day. When the representatives of the third estate, such as Robespierre, Marat and Danton, made known their ideas, which were to build a new society based on liberty and equality, the people supported them and made their revolution possible.

Who were the Jacobins?

After taking power and arresting the king, the representatives of the third estate met to decide on a new constitution, with new laws. Among them was a group led by Robespierre who wanted a complete and total change. This group was called the Jacobins.

Were they successful?

The ideas of Robespierre (pictured above) gained the upper hand but only for a short time. It was a tragic moment during the Revolution called the "Reign of Terror." All suspicious people were sent to the guillotine after a questioning process. Among the first victims was the king himself, who had tried to flee. The drawing on the left shows Louis XVI being sent to the guillotine.

How did the revolution end?

The harshness of Robespierre, who in one year condemned more than two thousand people to death, eventually disgusted even the revolutionaries, themselves. On July 27, 1794, they arrested Robespierre and sent him to the guillotine. The following year France created a new constitution.

Why was the revolution so important?

It was important because certain principles were triumphant which radically changed the conditions of society at that time, establishing the idea of the equality of all men before the state.

THE INDUSTRIAL REVOLUTION

What was the Industrial Revolution?
In England, in the second half of the eighteenth century, a new system of production was developed due to a series of technological innovations. This completely transformed social and economic relations not only in England but also all over Europe. This was known as the "Industrial Revolution."

What caused things to change?
The demand for manufactured goods and the spread of commerce was constantly growing. It drove men to think of new ways of production that would rely not just on people, whose work was slow and costly, but also on machines, which were constantly being improved.

What was the first industrial machine?
It was a mechanical loom, invented by the Englishman, John Kay. This machine was the start of the mechanization of weaving.

Who worked these machines?
Weaving had been done mostly by women who wove cloth on looms by hand (see linen weavers, pictured below). The new machines were operated by men who were organized in large shops that became the first factories.

What does "proletariat" mean?
The people who went to work in the first factories owned nothing. The only thing they had was the strength of their arms and a lot of children, or prole. When the children were old enough, they also went to work in the factories and mines, often at a very early age. In simplest terms, "proletariat" means the working class.

What kind of energy was used in heavy industry?
To work raw metal, very powerful sources of energy were needed that could move machinery like the steam hammer, pictured above. One source of this energy was steam.

Who invented the steam engine?
The first steam-driven piston, encased in a cylinder, was invented by James Watt in the second half of the eighteenth century. But it was only at the beginning of the next century that it was possible to create the forerunner of our modern blast furnaces, designed by another English engineer, James Naysmith.

Were there other uses for steam?
Yes. Steam was widely used in the field of transportation, both on water (steam boats) and on land (the first trains). Business grew increasingly competitive. As manufacturing increased, new factories were built and more energy was needed.

Did other sources of energy exist?
Coal had been used since ancient times, but beginning in the eighteenth century it became the most important source of energy. This fuel was used in factories until the discovery of oil. Pictured above is a coal pit.

What were the social consequences of the Industrial Revolution?
Factories grew up around coal fields and around large cities which provided a steady supply of workers. Men, women and children left the farms, lured by the possibility of a regular salary. Urban areas developed where at first people lived under miserable conditions and worked fourteen to sixteen hours a day. It was only at the end of the nineteenth century that workers organized themselves to defend their rights, and won shorter work days and better working conditions.

THE GREAT EXPLORERS

Who was Captain Cook?

James Cook was the most famous navigator after Columbus, Vasco da Gama and Magellan. His travels signaled the end of the great voyages of exploration to discover new lands and the beginning of scientific exploration.

In 1762 Cook sailed with the English navy to study the coasts of Newfoundland and Labrador. In 1768 he led an expedition to the South Pacific to observe the passage of the planet Venus across the sun. He then sailed around New Zealand, and continued on to map the east coast of Australia. He is also given credit for the discovery of the Easter Islands and Hawaii.

In 1776 he was sent to find the Northwest Passage, a route that connects the Atlantic with the Pacific. He reached the North American coast by way of Vancouver, then went north as far as the Bering Straits. But he could go no further as his way was blocked by ice.

What was the main purpose of the exploration of Africa?

In the late eighteenth century, scientific interest grew about the interior of Africa, which, until then was largely unknown. In 1798 the English founded the African Association whose purpose was to increase exploration. It wanted to discover the sources of the Nile and the Niger, as well as to cross the Sahara as far as the Niger.

Who were the great explorers of the African continent?

Between 1795 and 1805, the Scottish explorer, Mungo Park, carried out the first explorations of a scientific nature in the heart of the African continent. The German, Hornemann, went from Egypt to Fezzan between 1798 and 1800. He was the first to cross the Sahara from north to south. In 1822, Alexander Laing discovered the source of the Niger. The Englishman, Speke, discovered Lake Victoria and then its northern outlet, the Nile River. In 1864, Baker reached Lake Alberto-Nyanza, completing the exploration of the course of the river. The first real source of the Nile was discovered at the end of the century by an Austrian, Baumann. Southern Africa was explored by a Scottish missionary, David Livingstone, and an American, Henry Stanley, who are pictured below.

What were the major western explorations of the Asian continent?

From 1808 to 1812, the English explorers of the Asian Society discovered the sources of the Ganges and Indo Rivers. In 1833, a Scotsman, Burnes, crossed the Hindu Kush. Burma was explored by L. Fea and R. Colquhoun, in their search for a passage to China. In 1887, an Englishman, Younghusband, explored Manchuria and then crossed back to Beijing through central Asia from west to east. The highest mountains in the world, Everest (29,028 feet) and K2 (28,250 feet) were conquered in the twentieth century. In 1953, E. Hillary and his Nepalese guide, Tenzing, set foot on the highest peak in the world. The following year A. Compagnoni and L. Lacedelli conquered K2.

Before 1800

From 1800 to 1850

From 1850 to 1900

After 1900

EXPLORATION IN THE AFRICAN CONTINENT

Why was exploration of the Artic begun?

Initially it was to find passages that would link the Atlantic to the Pacific Ocean (the Northwest and the Northeast passages).

Who discovered the Northwest Passage?

Sir John Franklin was one of the first to lead a British expedition towards the Bering Straits. However, he was not able to cross it because his way was blocked by ice. Its complete navigation is credited to a Norwegian, Roald Amundsen, who, after three years, successfully crossed it in 1906.

Who discovered the Northeast Passage?

A Swede, Nordenskjold, was the first to cross it between 1878 and 1879.

Who was the first to reach the North Pole?

After many attempts by men such as Nansen and Johansen, Admiral Peary reached it on April 6, 1909.

Who conquered the South Pole?

On December 14, 1911, Amundsen's expedition placed the Norwegian flag there, thirty-four days ahead of the tragic expedition of an Englishman, Scott, who did not survive the journey.

THE AMERICAN CIVIL WAR

Who fought in the American Civil War?
The northern and southern states, which formed the nucleus of present-day America fought against each other in this war. The war lasted from 1861 to 1865. It came about as a result of diverse economic conditions. While the northern states already had an industrial base, the southern states based their economy on agriculture, and in particular, cotton.

Who fought against slavery?
The president of the new federation of the United States, Abraham Lincoln, fought for the freedom of the slaves. In his campaign, he declared that he was against slavery and resolved to abolish it if elected.

Who picked the cotton?
Blacks, who were bought in Africa as slaves like any other goods, were the ones who did most of the work on the immense cotton plantations. They were kept as slaves and their masters had complete power over their lives.

Why is the Civil War sometimes called "The War of Secession?"

After Lincoln won the election, seven Southern states voted to withdraw from the Union and form a separate confederacy in 1861. Shortly after, war broke out between the North and the South.

What happened during the war?

The Southern army, led by General Robert E. Lee, was at first the stronger. But after two years, two Northern Army officers, General Grant and General Sherman, after a long series of offensives, forced the retreat and surrender of the South. Among the many battles, there was a naval battle at Hampton Roads in Virginia between two great battleships, the Monitor for the North and the Virginian (formerly the Mer-

Why was this war important?

First of all, it made the northern states stronger. Because of them, industry spread to the new southern states. More important, perhaps, it put an end to slavery and reinforced the democratic principles that were at the base of American independence. Unfortunately, Lincoln was assassinated shortly following his success.

rimack) for the South. The North was the victor. This battle is illustrated below.

What were the results of the abolishment of slavery?

The Civil War finished one of the saddest pages in the history of man. But it opened another, even if involuntarily: that of racism. Although the laws stated that every American citizen had equal rights, regardless of the color of his skin, it was still difficult to eliminate from men's minds the idea of "differentness." Even after the abolition of slavery, acts of repression continued against Blacks. Such intolerance has continued until the present, not only in America, but in many other countries of the world, such as South Africa where a white minority still restricts the Black population to living in ghettos and doing the hardest jobs.

THE TWO WORLD WARS

When did the first World War start?
The European states started the first world conflict in 1914. On one side was the Austro-Hungarian Empire (Austria-Hungary and Germany) and on the other side, France, England and Russia, with Italy joining them in 1915.

Did America join it?
Yes, America declared war on Germany in 1917. When Germany declared unrestricted submarine warfare in neutral waters, the United States was forced to respond.

How long did the conflict last?
For five years, enemy troops were engaged in trench warfare. Trenches were an intricate maze of long narrow ditches, dug out as they went along by soldiers as they captured new territory. Sometimes enemy trenches were located only a few yards away. The soldiers used machine guns perched on the edge of the trenches. This is pictured below.

What other methods of combat did they use?
The first armored tanks, based on the Mark I, pictured above, were built during this war. These first tanks were improved and, along with the airplane, were the weapons most often used in the second World War.

When did World War II break out?
In 1939, the expansionist aims of Germany drew the world into a second bloody conflict. For six years Europe was at war again. This war brought about the destruction of many cities and the deaths of thousands of people. America joined England and France against Germany to bring it to an end. The Russians and the Italians were also involved. The Tiger, pictured above right, was Germany's most famous armored tank in World War II.

What kind of treaty did the great powers make at the end of the war?

Just before the end of the war, the Americans, the British and the Russians met in Yalta. There they decided how to divide up Germany when the war was over so that everyone would have a place to live and work. The representatives of the Yalta Declaration were Winston Churchill from Great Britain, Franklin Roosevelt from the United States and Joseph Stalin from the Soviet Union, pictured below.

What is the Cold War?

Since the end of the second World War, there have been many local wars between small countries. The great powers have also experienced times of great tension but instead of armed conflicts, these have resulted in "cold wars." This means that the great powers closed their markets and refused to sell their products to each other. This often produced great economic hardship.

What are the dangers of a new war?

Technology has improved greatly in the area of weapons. Missiles and bacterial warfare have been developed that can destroy vast agricultural areas, making them useless. But the greatest danger is that of nuclear weapons such as the atomic bomb which can destroy humanity in minutes.

Has the atomic bomb ever been used?

In Hiroshima, in August 1945, an atomic explosion completely destroyed an entire city in seconds and killed millions of people. It is a powerful example of the destructive capacity of this weapon.

DID YOU KNOW...?

What is the U.N.?
U.N. stands for the United Nations, created in 1945 with the goal of preserving world peace and security. It is located in New York. Its main bodies are the General Assembly, made up of all the member countries, the Security Council, the Economic and Social Council and the International Court of Justice, which is located in The Hague.

Who was Draco?
He was a legislator in Athens in the seventh century, B.C. He compiled the first written laws and was famous for the severity of his penalties.

Who was the first president of the United States?
He was George Washington, elected president in 1789.

Who was Bartolomeu Diaz?
He was a Portuguese navigator who was the first to reach the Cape of Good Hope at the southernmost tip of Africa in 1487.

Who founded the first settlement in America?
The Spanish set up the first permanent settlement in America in 1565. It was Saint Augustine in what is now the state of Florida.

Who were the Samurai?
They were the guards of the imperial palace in Japan until the end of the eleventh century. During the feudal period the samurai were the soldiers of the nobility.

Who was Benjamin Franklin?
He was an American statesman and scientist who lived in the eighteenth century. He was also a journalist and wrote *Poor Richard's Almanac*. Through his experiments with kites in lightning storms, he proved that lightning and electricity were identical.

What is the FAO?
FAO stands for the Food and Agriculture Organization, which was created in 1945 in Quebec. Today its headquarters are in Rome. It is concerned with the distribution of food in the world, especially in less developed areas.

Who were Lewis and Clark?
They were two American explorers who, from 1804-1806, mapped the land west of the Mississippi River, from Saint Louis to the Pacific Ocean, traveling over eight thousand miles.

What was the Mayflower?
It was the ship that, in 1620, brought the first English colonists, the Pilgrims, from England to North America. They landed at Plymouth Rock in Massachusetts on August 5, 1620.

Who were the Ming?
They were a dynasty of Chinese emperors who ruled from 1368 to 1644. Their reign was characterized by great artistic and intellectual development similar in importance to the European Renaissance.

What was the Minotaur?
It was a mythical monster with a human body and the head of a bull which lived on the island of Crete. It was kept shut up in a labyrinth in Minos and fed human sacrifices. It was finally killed by a young man, Theseus, with the help of Ariadne.

What are menhirs?
They are prehistoric monuments made up of huge stone slabs standing upright in the ground. Some can still be found in France, Great Britain and Italy.

What is "pluralism?"
It is a political state made up of many competing political parties, interest groups and ideological and cultural movements.

PLANTS AND ANIMALS

THE LIFE OF A PLANT

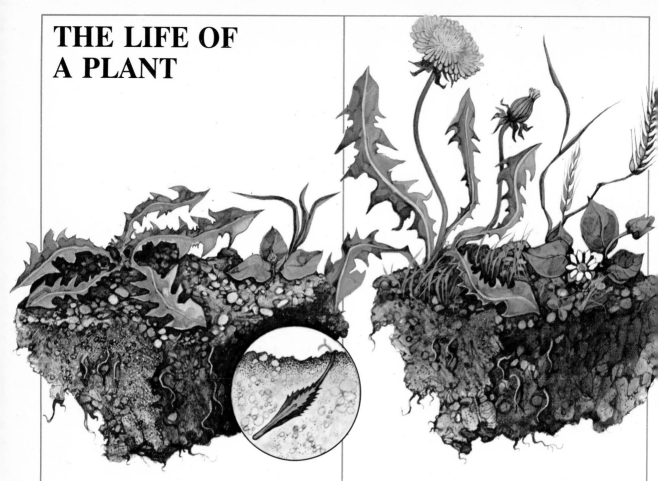

How does a plant grow?

Plants have a life cycle that can be divided into three different stages, from the time the seed takes root until it is a mature plant. First, there is germination, when the seed sprouts and produces roots, a stem and leaves. In the second stage the plant produces flowers which develop into seed-bearing fruit. In the last stage the fruit releases its seeds and the whole cycle begins again.

How long does a plant live?

Some plants, called annuals, carry out all the stages in their life cycle in a single year and then die. One example of an annual is the dandelion, shown above.

Others live longer. They are called biennials or perennials. All larger plants with woody stems are perennials. Once they reach maturity, they produce flowers and fruit and will do so regularly for the rest of their lives.

What is a dandelion?

The dandelion is a weed with yellow flowers, found mainly in fields and meadows. In the summer the flower becomes a downy ball of fluff which children like to blow on. The "fluff" contains the seeds which, carried by the wind, can fall to the ground a long way from the mother plant. During the winter, the seeds remain where the summer winds have blown them. In spring they germinate and grow into small plants with leaves arranged like a rosette around a flower bud. By summer the dandelions are in full bloom again. Then the little yellow flowers again change to become the downy seed-bearing fluff. Autumn brings the cycle to a close. The dandelions wither and die, having lived their entire life in the space of one year. But they leave behind their seeds, scattered over the meadows and fields, thus assuring the continuation of the plants the following spring.

What happens to perennials in the winter?

Unlike annuals, perennials do not die. They go into a dormant (resting) state in the cold weather.

When do perennials flower?

They generally flower in the spring. Some, like the geranium, form flowers beginning in the first year of life.

Others, like the peach tree, take three years before they produce the first flowers (illustrated at left).

There are also plants which learn to adapt to particularly difficult regions or situations. This happens to desert plants, such as the cactus, which can survive for long periods without water.

However, no plant can survive extended periods of drought.

second year

third year

first year

SEEDS

What do seeds do?

The seed is the ripened ovule of the fertilized ovary of the flower and the germ of a new plant. To survive, each plant must produce seeds that will germinate and continue the species. These seeds will grow into new plants with flowers, fruit and, eventually, more seeds, creating a continuous cycle of new life.

What do seeds consist of?

The essential part of the seed is the embryo since it contains a miniature future plant. Inside you can see a tiny root, the radicle, and stem, the hypocotyl which carries one or more seed leaves, or cotyledons and at the tip an embryonic bud, or plumule. The plant embryo is generally enveloped in the endosperm which contains its food reserve. The embryo is protected by a seed coat called the integument or testa. If there is no endosperm, the food supply comes from the cotyledons which will be swollen and fleshy, the way they are, i.e. in certain beans. The drawing below shows the sequence of germination of a castor oil plant.

What are gymnosperms and angiosperms?

The seed described above is an angiosperm. Gymnosperm means "bare seed." Unlike the angiosperm seed, the cotyledons of the gymnosperm are not enclosed in the fruit. Instead, the seed is protected by other organisms such as the scales of the pine cone. The conifer is an example of a gymnosperm.

How many cotyledons are there in a seed?

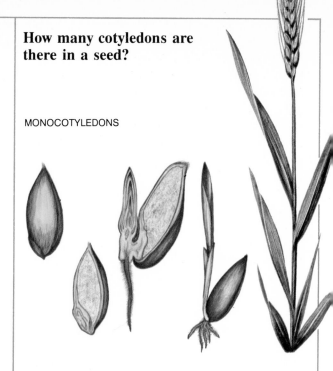

MONOCOTYLEDONS

A gymnosperm contains two or more cotyledons while the maximum number of cotyledons in an angiosperm is two. In the peanut, each half is a cotyledon. Angiosperms that have only one cotyledon are called monocotyledons. Some examples include: wheat, barley, corn and onions which are illustrated above.

Does the chemical makeup of seeds vary?

Yes, they vary according to their species. But all seeds are rich in oils, starches and proteins. Some seeds, like those of corn, peas, and onions, contain sugar as well. When these plants mature, the sugar changes into starch.

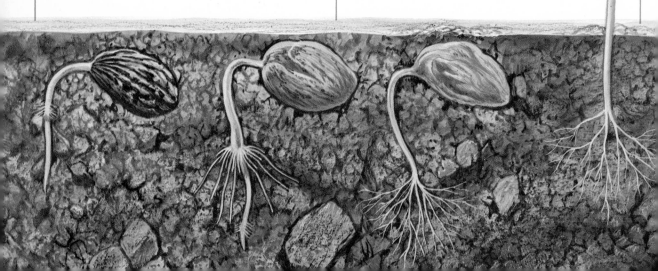

How are seeds used?

Seeds represent an important food reserve for the world. Think of cereals like wheat and rice or legumes like beans and peas. We get oils and margarines from soya, flax, sunflower and cotton seeds. Many spices also come from seeds: nutmeg, anise, mustard and cumin. Today, modern agricultural technology ensures quality control of seeds. This means they are checked to be sure that they are free from disease and have a good chance of germinating.

In the illustration at the right is a sunflower. Its seeds are very rich in oil, containing twenty-five to thirty-two per cent.

castor
oil plant

How big are seeds?

Seeds come in all sizes. They range from tiny ones not much bigger than a speck of dust to certain tropical orchids with seeds as big as coconuts.

How long can a seed "live?"

Some studies maintain that in exceptional cases, a seed can last indefinitely. But in reality the life of a seed varies from species to species. Some seeds, like those of the willow tree, must germinate as soon as they are released by the plant or they die.

The prize for longevity goes to the oriental lotus with its lovely pink flower. In the marshy peat bogs of Japan, some seeds of the lotus were discovered in a canoe dating back to Neolithic times. They had survived intact for more than two thousand years. Carefully tended by expert botanists, two of these seeds germinated and developed the splendid flower which is characteristic of the lotus.

DISSEMINATION

What is dissemination?
Dissemination is a phenomenon which results in the dispersal of seeds.
It can be active or passive.
In the first case, the plant itself scatters the seeds, sometimes near and sometimes far away. In the second, the seeds are scattered by the wind, water or by animals.

Why do plants need to spread their seeds?
If all the seeds a plant produced fell at its feet, very soon there would not be enough room for all of them to grow. This is why the plant tries to scatter its seeds over a wide area. They may be scattered with their fruit or alone.

How are seeds scattered away from the mother plant?
To travel a distance from the parent plant to a place where they will be able to germinate, seeds take advantage of the air, water and animals. In general their protective casing keeps them safe from damaging blows.

How does the water lily spread its seeds?
The water lily, like the coconut palm and the alder, is a plant that uses water to carry its seeds and fruit. The seeds of the water lily have a spongy covering with many air chambers. They allow the seed to float and travel considerable distances.

What characteristics do wind-borne seeds have?
Seeds carried by the wind may be very light, like those of the orchid and the digitalis, or they may have tiny wings, like the seeds of pines, ashes, elms and maples. Some, like the dandelion, the cotton plant, the willow and the poplar, come with hairy extensions that work like parachutes. Some of these special coverings and shapes not only allow the seed to float but also help them to stick to the coats of animals. You can see some of the wind-borne seeds below.

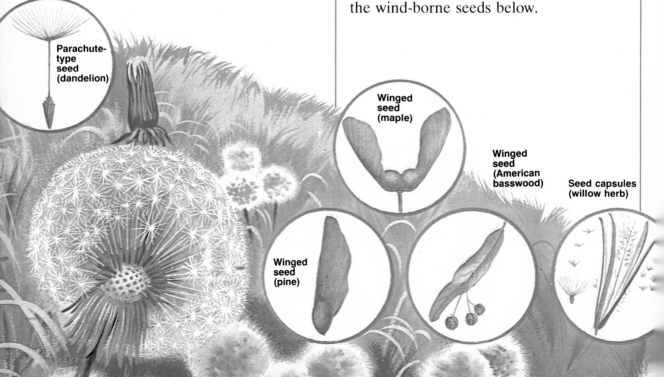

Parachute-type seed (dandelion)

Winged seed (maple)

Winged seed (American basswood)

Seed capsules (willow herb)

Winged seed (pine)

① ② ③ ④

How do animals help to scatter seeds?

Many plants keep their seeds inside colorful fleshy fruit to attract animals and make their dispersal easier.

As you can see in the illustration below, a goldfinch is dropping some of the seeds of the plant it is eating while a squirrel is carrying a nut away in its mouth and an ant is carrying a seed to its nest.

The seeds of certain plants become sticky when wet and cling to the feathers of birds and the fur of animals.

What other ways are seeds dispersed?

In some plants, like the poppy (1) and the snapdragon (2), the seeds are held in a capsule, or the fruit, that opens up. When the capsule is suspended, a light breeze is enough to jostle it and scatter the seeds.

Is it true that some fruits "explode" in order to disperse their seeds?

Yes, some seeds are shot out by an explosive mechanism. As the fruit dries, it begins to build up tension. Finally, the fruit bursts open, sending the seeds shooting off some distance from the mother plant. It is a method used by legumes such as the pea. A similar mechanism is also used by the violet (3) and the balsam (4).

Why do some fruits have burrs?

Burrs enable them to attach themselves to the fur of animals. The fruit of certain grasses, for example, has tiny hooks that get caught in the fur of sheep, so that they may end up being carried considerable distances.

LEAVES

What is the inside of a leaf like?
The outer surface of a leaf is protected by a very fine layer, the cuticle. This outer epidermis, or covering, lets sunlight through but protects the plant from water evaporation.
Under this layer are layers of tissue that make up the parenchyma. Their cells, rich in chloroplasts, are where photosynthesis takes place.
Below them are other cells, the mesophyll, which have space around them that allows air to circulate.
Finally, there are openings called stoma where gases are exchanged between the plant and the atmosphere.

What is photosynthesis?
It is a process that is the result of a long series of chemical reactions which lets the plant produce the substances necessary for its nutrition. To simplify it, one could say that it is the synthesis of carbon dioxide (CO_2) and water (H_2O) in simple sugars like glucose. During this process, oxygen (O_2) is released through the stoma.

What is chlorophyll?
It is a green pigment, found in the cell, that can change light energy into chemical energy. This permits the development of the process of photosynthesis.
Through the pores in its leaf the plant absorbs molecules of carbon dioxide from the air, while through its roots, it receives molecules of water that have accumulated in the layer of cells in the parenchyma.
As soon as the tiniest amount of solar energy reaches the leaf, it is intercepted by the chlorophyll and transformed into chemical energy.

Do plants breathe?
Like all living things, plants breathe, too. In their case, this means that oxygen is taken in and carbon dioxide is expelled. The gases travel throughout the plant, entering and leaving by means of the many stoma on the underside of the leaf. This process is known as respiration.

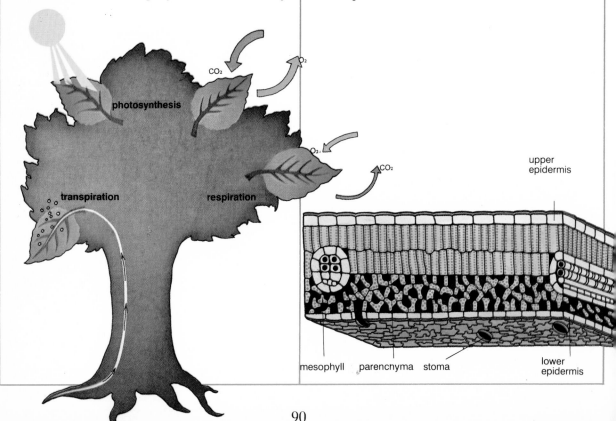

Leaf shapes

hastate
(sheep's sorrel)

obovate
(willow)

elliptic
(rose)

saggitate
(arrowhead)

serrate
(chestnut)

linear
(pine)

lobate
(oak)

What is transpiration?

In order to nourish itself, a plant will absorb a large mineral-rich quantity of water (more than it needs) through its roots. It then eliminates the excess water through the stoma in the leaves. The stoma are furnished with a kind of cover which regulates the amount of water released so that they do not dry out. This process is called transpiration.

Why do leaves fall?

When the temperature drops below a certain point, the absorption of water by the roots of a plant or tree decreases considerably, until it stops altogether. If the leaves were to continue to transpire, the plant would dry out completely. Because of this the substances contained in the leaves drain away and accumulate within the bark or the stalk. The dry and useless leaf is now ready to fall from the tree or plant. But before it does, the plant forms a kind of scar at the point where the leaf is attached to the branch so that once it falls, there is no open wound.

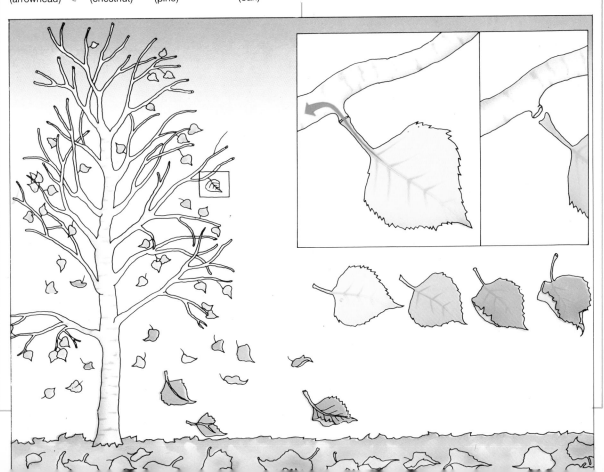

THE STEM

What is a stem?
The stem is the part of the plant that, in most cases, grows up into the air and supports the branches and leaves.

Why does a plant need a stem?
The stem is a connecter between the roots, which absorb water from the soil, and the leaves, which carry out photosynthesis.

What is a trunk?
The trunk is the hard woody stem of plants with branches, like the oak or the fir.

What is bark?
Bark is one of the layers that make up the trunk. Because it is the outermost layer, it protects the tree.

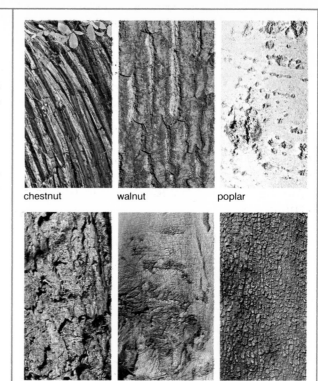

chestnut   walnut   poplar

larch   beech   holm oak

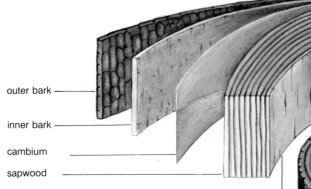

outer bark

inner bark

cambium

sapwood

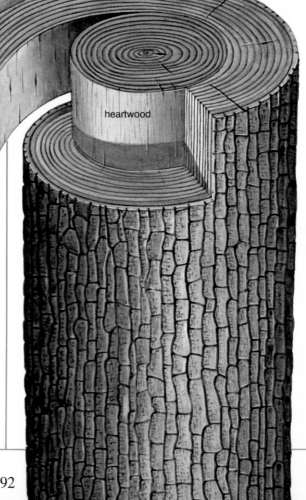

heartwood

How many layers does a trunk have?
As you can see in the illustration on the right, there are five layers in the trunk. The innermost layer, the heartwood, is often hard and gives the trunk the strength to hold up the foliage. The sapwood, made up of vessels through which the sap travels from the roots to the leaves is next. Next there is a very thin layer between the sapwood and inner bark called the cambium. The inner bark is made up of the vessels through which the sap is carried from the leaves to the other organs of the plant. Finally, there is the outer bark, the layer visible to us, which protects the trunk.

Are there other kinds of stems?

Yes. Besides trunks there are many other types of stems. For example, the stem of a palm tree is a very woody stalk without branches. Grains, like wheat, rice and rye and many grasses have strong, hollow stems. Other plants, like clover, have solid stems. The cactus has a stem that serves both as a water reservoir as well as the part which carries out the function of chlorophyll production. Its leaves are reduced to spines.

Are there climbing as well as creeping stems?

Yes. Many plants have stems that cannot stand upright without support. Some, like the strawberry plant, creep over the surface of the ground while others, like the grapevine or the honeysuckle, attach themselves to supports, using curly tendrils. Still others, like the bean plant, wrap themselves around another plant.

Do all stems grow upwards?

No. Many plants have underground stems that never see the light at all. These strange subterranean stems look like roots, although they aren't. Sometimes they grow very big, accumulating large reserves of food that they use in the spring to nourish new plants.

Are there many types of subterranean stems?

There are three kinds of subterranean stems: the rhizome, the tuber and the bulb. The rizhome is a long stem that lies close to the surface of the soil and grows horizontally. The lily of the valley and the iris both have rhizomes. The tuber is a branch that grows down into the ground. As it grows, it produces a sugary substance, starch. A typical example of a tuber is the potato. The bulb has a very short stem that is enclosed and protected by fleshy leaves, as in the case of the onion and the tulip.

Do all plants have stems?

Only vascular plants, those with vessels to carry sap, have stems. Mosses, fungi, algae and bacteria are not vascular plants and therefore do not have stems.

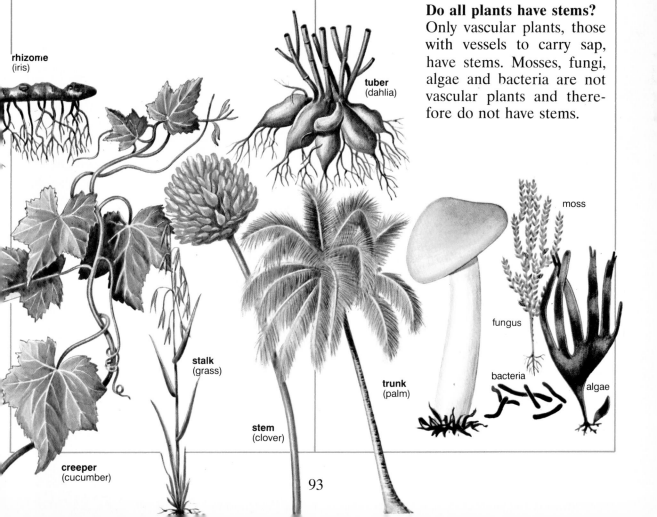

rhizome
(iris)

tuber
(dahlia)

moss

fungus

stalk
(grass)

trunk
(palm)

bacteria

algae

stem
(clover)

creeper
(cucumber)

RECORD-BREAKING PLANTS

Do plants compete with each other?
We often speak of the fastest runner, the best actor or singer, the strongest weight lifter. To be the best at something is an achievement to man, resulting in stiff competition. In nature, too, records are set, but without the competitive spirit of man.

What is the tallest tree in the world?
The sequoia is the tallest tree. Some sequoias have reached heights of more than two hundred sixty feet with trunks almost thirty feet in diameter.

How long can a plant live?
The life span of a plant varies widely. Wheat, for example, is sown in autumn and if it is not harvested the following summer, it will wither and die. Peas, beans and pumpkins sprout, grow and die in just a few months. This happens to many herbaceous plants that do not have woody stems. On the other hand, there are trees that can live for more than a thousand years. The birch tree only lives for one-hundred to one-hundred-twenty years but the giant sequoia can live for close to four thousand years!

Which trees live the longest?
Besides the sequoia, there are the common cypress (three thousand years), the chestnut (two thousand years) and the cedar of Lebanon (twelve hundred years). The oak, noted for its longevity, lives only five to seven hundred years.

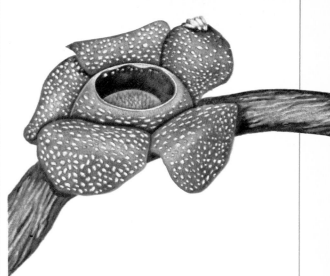

What tree holds the record for being the oldest tree?

There are specimens of the bristolcone pine (pictured above is a drawing of its cone), in the forests of North America, that are over forty-six hundred years old.

How can you tell the age of a tree?

In its first year of life, the trunk of a tree develops a woody ring that grows around the pith. Each year the tree adds another ring. When the tree is cut down, you can count the number of rings in order to figure out the age of the tree. The above left picture shows an example of these rings.

Which plant grows at the highest altitude?

During a climb up the second-highest mountain in the world, K2 in the Himalayan chain, a red lichen (Xanthoria elegans) was found at about 21,600 feet. In the Alps, the record for the plant growing at the highest altitude goes to the ranunculus, a buttercup-like flower that has been found at over 13,000 feet in the Swiss Alps.

Which plant "drinks" the most?

A climber belonging to the palm family, the rattan plant can stretch more than six hundred fifty feet. If you cut a piece six to ten feet long, more than two pints of clear, drinkable water that the plant has sucked up through its roots will pour out.

Are there any record-holding flowers?

Yes, the corpse lily (above), from the Rafflesiaceae family, is a parasitic plant that lives on the stems and roots of woody tropical forest plants. These flowers grow up to a yard in diameter and can weigh as much as eighteen pounds.

How long can the roots of a plant grow?

Roots can develop under or above the ground. The desert tamarisk, for example, can grow down more than one hundred sixty feet when in search of water. The roots of the banyan tree, an East Indian fig tree, has long aerial roots that grow down from the branches and help support the tree. One old tree in Calcutta has two hundred thirty prop roots around a forty foot trunk.

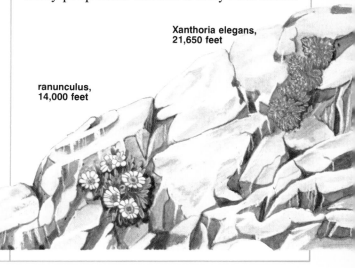

Xanthoria elegans,
21,650 feet

ranunculus,
14,000 feet

POLLINATION

petals

Why do plants have flowers?
Flowers carry on the process of reproduction in plants. In an angiosperm the flower contains the reproductive organs, which are divided into two parts. One part, the stamen, consists of a thin filament supporting the anther. The other part, the pistil, is made up of the ovary and the stigma which receives the pollen.

How are new seeds made?
Grains of pollen are transferred from the stamen to the pistil of the flower, this is called pollination. They are then carried down to the ovary which is fertilization.

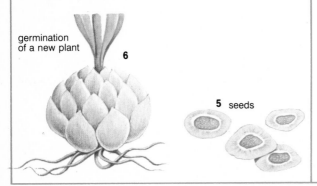

germination of a new plant

6

5 seeds

How is the pollen carried from the stamen to the pistil?
Pollination takes place with help from the wind or animals. In some cases, even water can be a carrier of the pollen.

How does fertilization happen?
In the illustration below, we can follow the stages in the formation of a new plant.
1. Each stamen has an anther that releases pollen when it is mature. 2. The released pollen is carried to the pistil and sticks to the stigma. 3. The pollen then passes through the style and reaches the ovules where fertilization takes place. 4. The ovary develops into fruit which contains the seeds of the fertilized ovules (5). 6. If conditions are right, new plants will develop from these seeds. When they mature, new flowers will blossom and the cycle will be repeated.

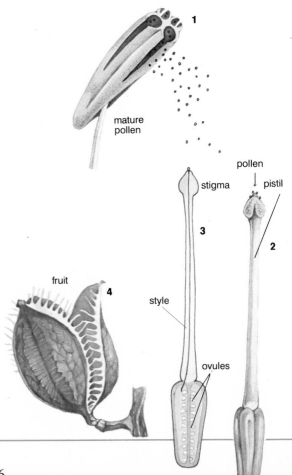

mature pollen

1

pollen

stigma

pistil

3

2

fruit

4

style

ovules

What are the different kinds of pollination?

There are wind, animal and water pollination. Plants pollinated by the wind produce large quantities of very light dry pollen that is easily carried by the air. In the illustration below, you can see an example of wind pollination of a gymnosperm (pine and fir trees) with inconspicuous unisex flowers. Insect pollination happens when the pollen has a surface that is spiny or sticky so that it adheres to animals or insects. Some plants, like Scotch broom, only release their pollen to certain insects. Insects are among the best carriers of pollen, particularly bumblebees and butterflies, who get nourishment from the nectar, a sugary substance that collects in the calyx of the flower. Flowers use many devices to attract pollinators. Rich scents and colorful flowers are irresistible to some insects. To penetrate the calyx, the little insects must push their way in to the anther, which when mature, will release its pollen.

The pollinators, traveling from flower to flower, carry the pollen with them, then leave it behind, dusting the stigma of the pistil with it.

Plants using water pollination generally produce a huge amount of pollen that is wrapped in a water-resistant membrane.

How many kinds of plant fertilization are there?

Some flowers have both stamen and pistils in the same plant where the whole process takes place. This is called "self-fertilization."

Other plants have stamen in one plant and pistils in another. In this case pollen must be carried from one plant to another, called "cross-fertilization."

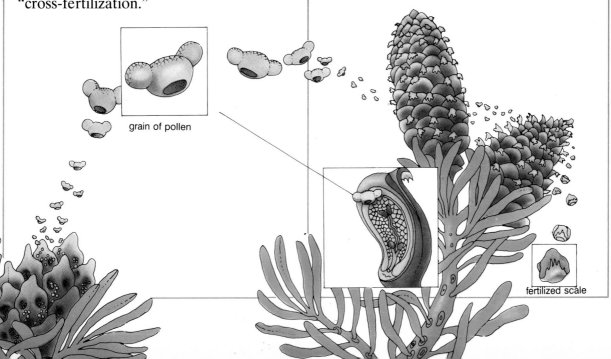

grain of pollen

fertilized scale

STRANGE PLANTS AND FLOWERS

How do plants get nourishment?
A special substance in most plants, chlorophyll, plays a very important part in their nourishment intake. It allows the plant to absorb sunlight which is necessary for the transformation of light energy into chemical energy, called photosynthesis, to occur. However, there are some plants which cannot get their nourishment this way and instead must get their food from other plants. These plants are called "parasites" and the plants on which they attach themselves are called "host plants." In some cases there is a mutal benefit to both the host and the parasite. When this happens, we say they live in symbiosis.

Do parasite plants produce flowers?
Generally they do not. But some of these strange plants produce very beautiful flowers, like the orchid or the mistletoe. This happens because they are not entirely parasitic.

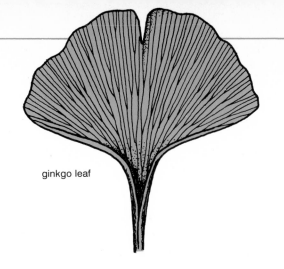

ginkgo leaf

How does the mistletoe live?
The mistletoe is a shrub that grows on apple, pear, poplar, almond and plum trees. It has long fleshy leaves through which it can produce at least some of its own nourishment. It gets the rest by living off its host plant as illustrated below.

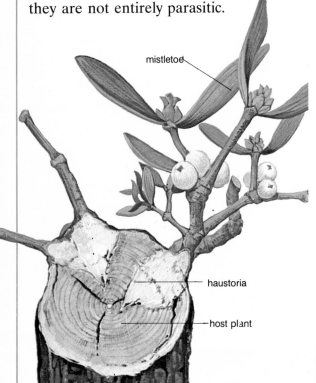

mistletoe

haustoria

host plant

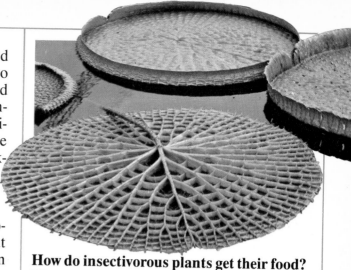

When did plants develop leaves?

Once, millions of years ago, all plants lived in the water. When they began to change to life on land, their branches grew closer and became flatter and a thin skin formed connecting them. These were the first rudimentary leaves and we can still admire them today in an ancient plant like the ginkgo (above left).

Are all orchids parasites?

No. Some are true parasites or "saprophytic," living on decaying plants, but others are "epiphytic" and only grow on other trees for support (opposite page, right).

Is there such things as floating plants?

The water lily with its strong acquatic roots seems to float. The most spectacular is the "Victoria," which grows more than six feet in diameter (above right).

How do insectivorous plants get their food?

These plants have flowers which can capture and digest small insects. A bee, attracted by a flower's perfume, lands on its oily surface and slips down inside it. Then the mouth of the flower closes over the insect, creating a deadly trap such as that of the pitcher plant, illustrated below left.

The Venus flytrap uses a special mechanism to catch its food. Its leaves have tiny tentacles that close around an insect as soon as it comes in contact with it. Then an acidic liquid is released which digests the animal (below).

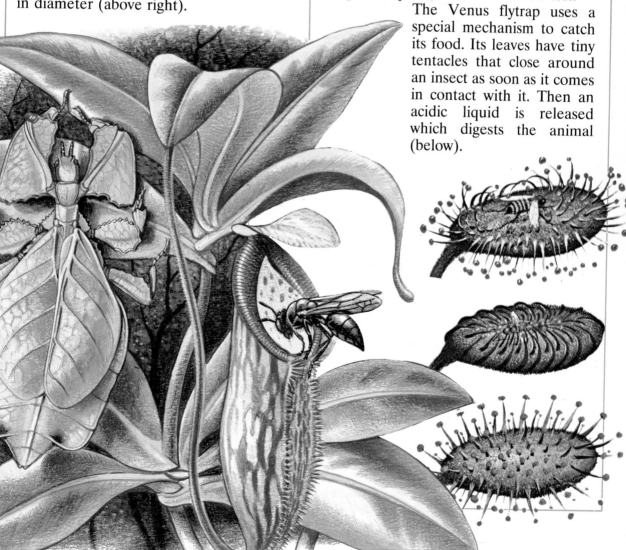

FRUIT

What is fruit?
Fruit comes from the transformation of the ovary of a flower after fertilization. The ovary protects and nourishes the seeds until they are ripe and then helps with their dispersal. Different fruits do this in different ways.

There are many kinds of fruit. Not only are peaches, cherries and bananas fruit, but also pumpkins, grains of wheat and pea pods.

How are fruits classified?
The first distinction we can make with a fruit is whether or not it opens to release its seeds when it is ripe. If it does, it is called "dry dehiscent;" if it does not, it is called "indehiscent."

We can also divide fruit by whether it is fleshy and juicy or hard and dry. Another way is to look at how the fruit grows. If it comes in bunches made up of smaller fruit, it is called "collective."

There are also true and false fruits, according to changes in the ovary or other parts of the flower, such as the receptacle tissue. This is the case with apples and pears.

What is the "pericarp?"
The "pericarp" is the part of the fruit that surrounds the seeds. It can have as many as three different layers. The outermost layer is the "epicarp" (for example, the skin of a cherry). The middle layer is the "mesocarp" (the flesh of a cherry) and the inner layer closest to the seed is the "endocarp" (the hard outer seed cover).

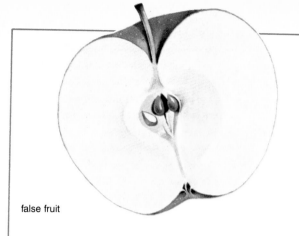

false fruit

berries

Why is the apple considered to be a false fruit?

Because it is the receptacle, and not the ovary of the apple that has grown and become fleshy, forming a pulp. The true fruit or ovary is actually what we call the core of the apple.

Which are the "indehiscent" fruits?

The main group is the achene which has a thin resistant pericarp containing a single seed. Some typical achenes are the sunflower and the carrot. Nuts, like the hazel nut, enclose their seed inside an extremely hard pericarp. Another group, the drupe, has truly stone-like fruit (the pits of the cherry, olive, peach and plum). The caryopsis, or true grain, has only one seed with a pericarp that is virtually inseparable from it. The samara, typified by the elm, maple and ash, has fruit with a woody pericarp and a winglike growth containing the seed.

Which fruits are "dry dehiscent?"

Many of the legumes, or podded fruits are considered to be "dry dehiscent." They have two chambers that carry the seeds, such as those found in peas and beans. The silique, typical of the mustard plant, has an ovary with two chambers. Another group which includes the poppy, has a capsule with two or more chambers.

legume or pea pod

Which fruits are considered "fleshy?"

The drupe is a fleshy fruit containing a single seed enclosed in a leathery endocarp. The cherry, peach and apricot are drupes. Another kind of fleshy fruit is the berry, with a very soft epicarp, a pulpy mesocarp and an endocarp with lots of seeds. Tomatoes, grapes and blueberries are considered true berries. Two specialized types of berries are the pepo and the hesperidium. The pepo group, that includes cucumbers and pumpkins, has a tough outer layer of pericarp and a softer endocarp and mesocarp full of seeds. The hesperidia category includes citrus fruits.

multiple fruit

What is an infructescence?

An infructescence is a cluster of fruit produced by the flowering of an inflorescence, or cluster of flowers. The whole cluster of fruit appears to be one single fruit, as is the case with mulberries or figs. But, an infructescence is different from multiple fruit because in the latter, the individual fruits come from different pistils of a single flower, as is the case with the blackberry (above), the raspberry and the strawberry.

NUTS

What are nuts?

Normally, we classify hazel nuts and other dry fruit such as chestnuts, as well as pine nuts and peanuts as nuts. But actually pine nuts are not fruit but rather, seeds and the peanut is a vegetable. Therefore, we will consider true nuts only those hard-shelled fruits that develop from two or more chambers (the organs that carry the seed) and that do not open when they are ripe.

What does a nut consist of?

True nuts have a fleshy outer layer, a woody shell and a center containing an edible cotyledon. These cotyledons are called kernels and they are the part that we use to make oils.

Which nut is the biggest?

The coconut, a member of the drupe family, is the biggest, weighing in at about four pounds and measuring eight to twelve inches in diameter. Its inner cavity is filled with a sweet whitish liquid called coconut milk. We extract oils and vegetable butters from coconuts.

What are the characteristics of a walnut?

A walnut, with a scientific name of "Juglans regia," is a monoecious plant, meaning it has both male and female flowers. The male flowers are grouped together as catkins, inflorescent penules about four inches long. The female flowers are either single or in small groups of two to four flowers. The fruit of the walnut, drupe, consists of a two-layered shell. The outer layer, the esocarp, is green and soft when immature and black when ripe. The inner layer, the endocarp, a woody bivalve, encloses the kernel. The wood of the walnut tree is used in furniture making.

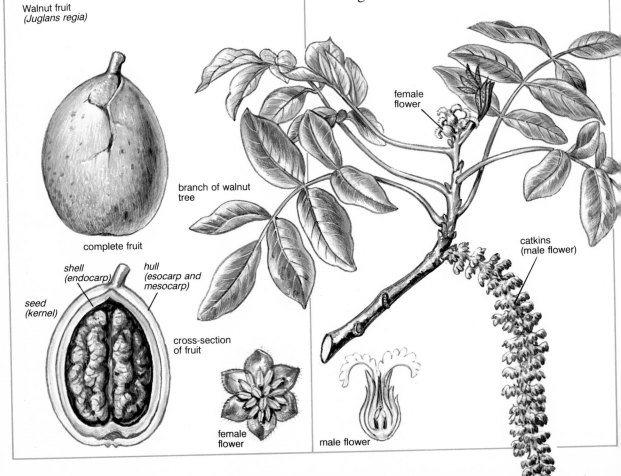

Walnut fruit
(Juglans regia)

complete fruit

shell
(endocarp)

hull
(esocarp and
mesocarp)

seed
(kernel)

cross-section
of fruit

female
flower

branch of walnut
tree

female
flower

catkins
(male flower)

male flower

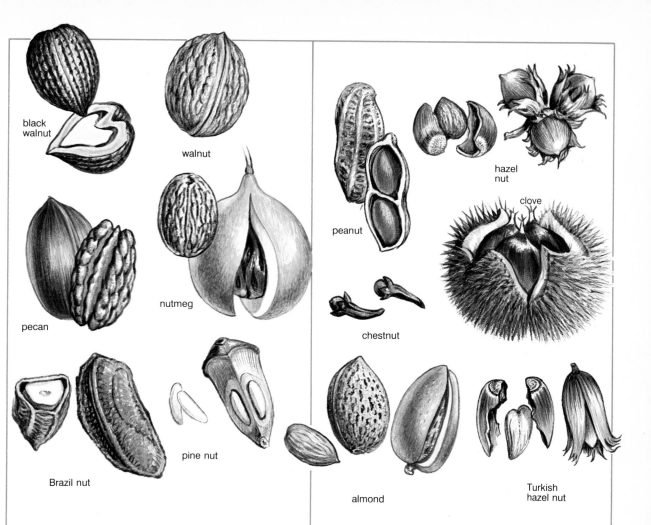

black walnut

walnut

pecan

nutmeg

Brazil nut

pine nut

peanut

hazel nut

clove

chestnut

almond

Turkish hazel nut

Where do nuts grow?

Nuts are cultivated in many tropical, subtropical and temperate regions. The almond, a native of Asia, is found today in many Mediterranean countries as well as California. The chestnut grew all over Europe, Africa, Asia and in the eastern part of the United States. Because the American chestnut was struck by disease, today there are not many to be found there. The hazel nut grows in Mediterranean countries and in the American Northeast. The peanut, originally from Brazil, can still be found today in India, China, Africa and the United States. The clove, usually thought of as a spice, is from the Moluccas. The pistachio is native to warm and temperate zones. The Brazil nut comes from the Amazon River basin and its giant evergreen trees grow wild in Brazil and Bolivia.

Do nuts have much nutritional value?

Nuts have a high vitamin, protein, and fat content and also contain many minerals. This makes them a very important source of nutrition. Many nuts are used in baking, as an ingredient in pies, puddings and ice creams, while others can be added to soups and stews. Some of them are made into cooking oils or used as flavorings or even spices.

Are nuts also used in industry?

Strychnine, used in the pharmaceutical industry, is extracted from the seeds of the "nux vomica," a nut that grows in the forests of India and Burma. The nuts of some fruits are crushed and used as filling in the production of plastics. Some nuts are used to make buttons, while others go into the manufacture of inks, paints, varnishes and cosmetics.

THE MEADOW

What is a meadow?
We usually think of a meadow as a large area covered by short grasses and simple flowers. In fact, it is a community of plants and animals and its fertility depends upon their balance.

Are there both natural and artificial meadows?
There are very few natural meadows left anymore, if you do not count those high up in the mountains. But there are many artificial meadows. These are meadows that farmers mow and fertilize periodically so they can harvest food for their animals.

How are meadows useful?
Because of their humidity, meadows cool the atmosphere, nourish the soil and help prevent the development of landslides and earth cave-ins.

How can a meadow "nourish" the soil?
Plants and grasses need constant and abundant nourishment, which they absorb through their roots. Every year the roots are replaced; the old ones, when they decompose, provide nourishment for a whole range of microorganisms. They, in turn, create humus, which is a thin layer of very fertile soil.

What does grass need in order to grow?
The presence of phosphorous favors the development of roots, while potassium protects them from illness and helps in the absorption of nutriments.

What are microorganisms?
They are very tiny simple organisms that help with the decomposition of animal and vegetable matter that form humus.

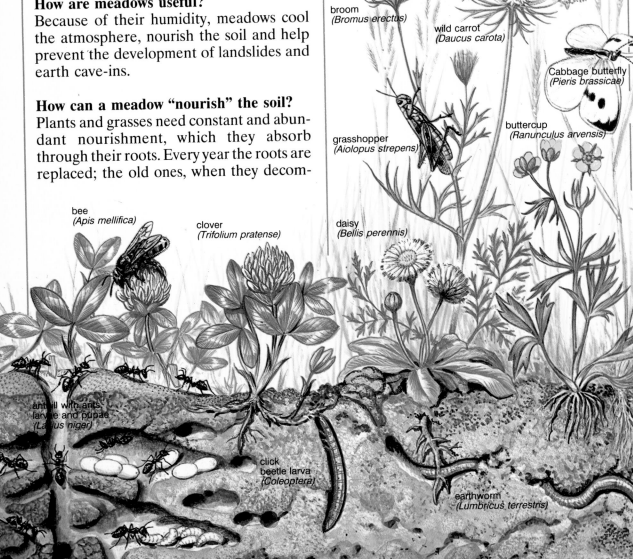

broom
(Bromus erectus)

wild carrot
(Daucus carota)

Cabbage butterfly
(Pieris brassicae)

grasshopper
(Aiolopus strepens)

buttercup
(Ranunculus arvensis)

bee
(Apis mellifica)

clover
(Trifolium pratense)

daisy
(Bellis perennis)

anthill with ants
larvae and pupae
(Lasius niger)

click
beetle larva
(Coleoptera)

earthworm
(Lumbricus terrestris)

What else lives in a meadow?

There are many living things there, some of which are useful and others which are very harmful. In the helpful group, the earthworm plays a very important role by helping the soil to breathe. The tunnels it continuously digs out help to break up the earth in areas where it is very compact. In the harmful group are the leaf eaters like the grasshopper and the maggot which eat the roots of plants. Ecologically speaking, however, all of these organisms are needed to maintain an ecological balance.

Are all meadows the same?

Meadows are different according to the way they are used. For example, how dense the grass is, how often it is cut and how resistant it is to weeds all determine what kind of meadow it will be.

Can you create a meadow?

Many experiments have been carried out so that today farmers can grow grasses and plants suitable for the climate they will grow in and for the way they will be used.

Is mowing useful?

Mowing a meadow generally helps to prevent the growth of weeds. Unlike grasses, weeds grow from the tip upwards and this is the part eliminated with mowing. Grasses, which grow from the base, will continue to develop since mowing only eliminates the tip. Mowing a meadow is useful for farmers because it produces fodder (food) for their animals.

Do meadows need water?

A meadow should always be kept humid, but not overly so. Too much water encourages fungus to develop, which is harmful to the grasses.

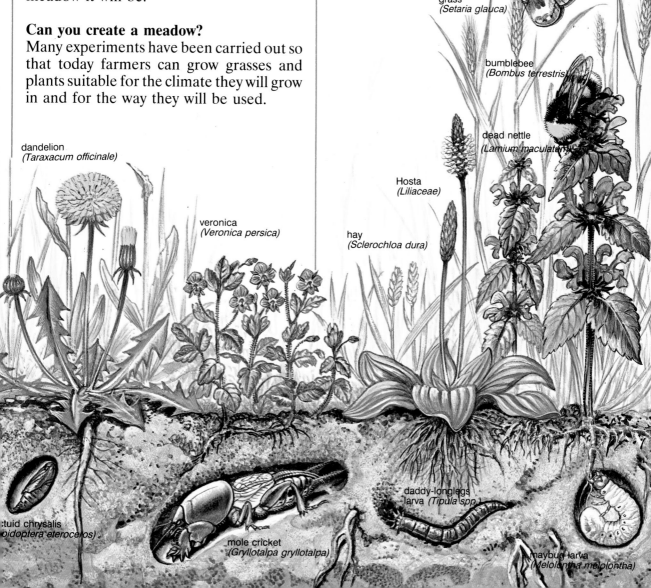

butterfly
(Coenonympha pamphilus)

grass
(Setaria glauca)

bumblebee
(Bombus terrestris)

dead nettle
(Lamium maculatum)

Hosta
(Liliaceae)

dandelion
(Taraxacum officinale)

veronica
(Veronica persica)

hay
(Sclerochloa dura)

daddy-longlegs
larva (Tipula spp.)

ctuid chrysalis
oidoptera eterocelos)

mole cricket
(Gryllotalpa gryllotalpa)

maybug larva
(Melolontha melolontha)

MUSHROOMS AND FUNGI

What are mushrooms and fungi?

They are plants that lack chlorophyll and so must live off other plants. They get their nutrients from organic material that has been produced by other living organisms (parasite mushrooms) or from the remains of dead organisms (saprophyte mushrooms) or they live in symbiosis with other organisms. The part of the mushroom that pokes up through the soil is the edible part. The vegetative part of the mushroom, the mycelium, or spawn, lies hidden in the earth and consists of very fine interwoven filaments that absorb water and other dissolved substances.

What is "mycorrhiza?"

It is a special form of symbiosis between a fungus and a tree. In some species the spawn of the mushroom penetrates into the roots of the tree and takes the place of its root hairs, sucking up water from the earth for both the fungus and the tree. In return, the plant gives the fungus a part of the organic substance it produces, thus supplying the fungus with nutrients.

Are there microscopic fungi?

Yes. Thousands of fungi are invisible to the naked eye. The mould that forms on fruits and vegetables is a kind of microscopic fungi. Yeast is another microscopic fungus that we have known about and used since ancient times. One kind, brewer's yeast, is used in baking to make bread rise.

How do mushrooms reproduce?

The seeds of the mushroom are called spores. They are tiny lightweight granules that are on the underside of the mushroom cap. When the mushroom is mature, the spores fall to the ground, germinate and produce the filaments that make up the mycelium. The mycelium, or spawn, spreads and grows and new fruit develops from it. When the new fruit reaches maturity, it drops new spores and the cycle starts again. Every mushroom produces thousands of spores.

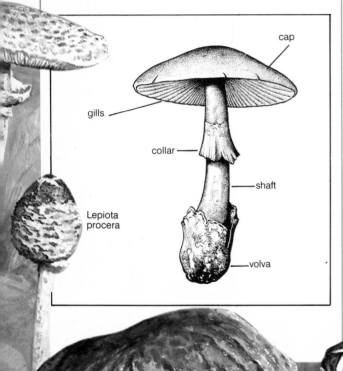

cap

gills

collar

shaft

Lepiota
procera

volva

Boletus
edulis

Boletus
scaber

Excellent mushrooms are found around trees because a kind of mutualism forms between the tree roots and the mushrooms. In the drawing, spores falling from the mushroom will create new spawn which will produce new plants.

enlarged spawn

spawn

Auricularia

Which mushrooms are edible?

The best-known edible mushrooms include: the ordinary mushroom that we are most familiar with, Agaricus bisporus; the porcini, Boletus edulis; the oyster mushroom used in oriental cooking, Pleurotus ostreatus; the garden mushroom, Agaricus. campestris; the chanterelle, Cantherellus cibarius; and the morel, Morchella esculenta.

Which mushrooms are poisonous?

Some mushrooms are extremely poisonous and even fatal if eaten. Members of the Amanita family are the most dangerous (Amanita muscaria, or fly agaric, Amanita phalloides, or the death cup, and Amanita virosa). Another poisonous mushroom is Cortinarius orellanus.

Are mushrooms useful?

They certainly are, because to get nourishment, they break down dead plants and leaves that cover the forest floor. They also get rid of other organisms and release carbon dioxide into the air, as well as mineral substances into the soil which become nutrients for other plants.

Armillaria or
Armillaria mellea

Agaricus
hortensis

Morchella
esculenta

CULTIVATED PLANTS

Can plants be "domesticated?"

Fruit trees, the vegetables in our vegetable gardens, ornamental flowers, such plants as cotton and hemp whose fibers we use to make clothing – in short – all the plants we cultivate today, once grew wild. Man has modified or adapted them to meet his needs, just as he did with animals. First, he eliminated the plants that were not useful to make room for those that were. Once he knew more about their habits, he modified them to make them produce as much as possible, to protect them from disease and to help them adapt to different climates. This was so successful that today some plants, such as corn, barely resemble their ancestors at all.

Where do domestic plants come from?

The plants that we grow today often originally came from places very far away. Rice, for example, was a native of East Asia. Corn, potatoes, tomatoes and beans came from the Americas and spread all over the world, while figs first grew in Arabia.

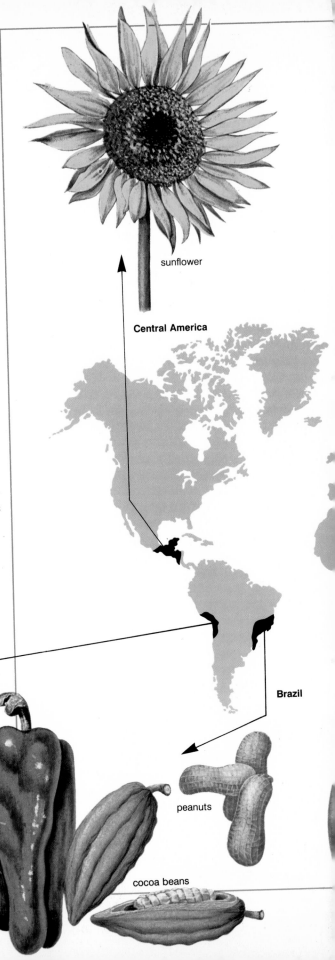

sunflower

Central America

Peruvian Andes

peppers

Brazil

peanuts

cocoa beans

potato

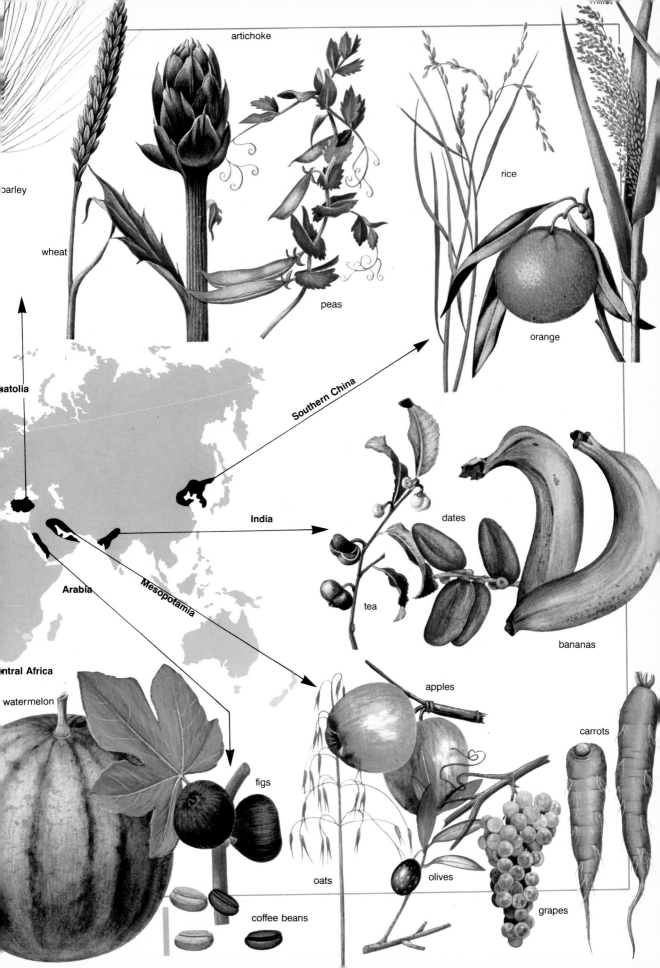

artichoke

barley

wheat

peas

rice

orange

Anatolia

Southern China

India

Arabia

Mesopotamia

Central Africa

watermelon

tea

dates

bananas

figs

apples

carrots

oats

olives

grapes

coffee beans

ANIMAL LOCOMOTION

Do four-legged animals move in many different ways?

Yes. For example, when an animal like a giraffe walks, it moves the two feet on one side forward simultaneously. This gait is called an amble. Dogs often move at a march, raising one foreleg and the opposite hindleg at the same time. When a horse gallops, there are moments when none of his four legs are touching the ground.

How do reptiles move?

Typically they move by waving their body and tail. This is true even of the lizard. Although they have tiny feet, they use them mostly for support and not for movement. A snake moves through its hole with an accordion-like movement, pulling in its body and then springing forward. Some desert snakes try to reduce their contact with the hot desert sand by rolling their bodies along sideways in a movement called sidewinding.

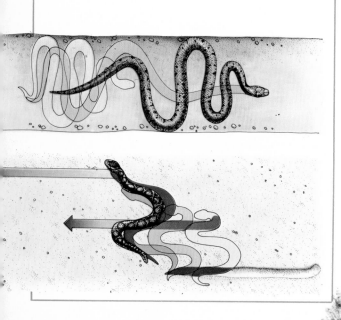

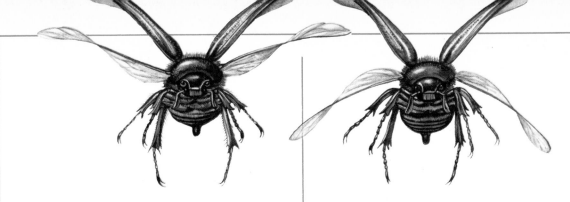

Do birds and insects have different kinds of wings?

There are three kinds of animal wings. The wings of a bird are actually similar to the

forelegs of land animals, even though they are covered with feathers and quills. The wings of an insect, however, are made of a delicate transparent membrane. The wings of a bat are also made of a thin membrane but it is stretched between the body and the fingers of the forearm.

How do birds fly?

The drawing above shows the flight of a pigeon. The bird starts off with a jump and then rapidly begins to beat its wings to pick up speed. Often, when it has reached a certain velocity, it no longer needs to flap its wings. Then it spreads them wide and glides through the air in free flight, using very little energy. Some birds use free flight to take advantage of rising air currents, letting themselves be carried up with very little effort on their part.

Do beetles use their wings to fly?

Yes. Before taking off, they raise their hard forewings and keep them immobile while their back wings begin to vibrate. The tips move in a figure-eight-like pattern and act somewhat like the propellers of an airplane.

How far can a frog jump?

A frog can jump almost a yard at a time. This corresponds to about twelve times the length of its body. The kangaroo can jump distances equal to five times its height. It does not hold the jumping record among animals, however. This goes to the tiny flea who can jump two hundred times its height.

How does a frog jump?

The jump of a frog begins with a powerful lunge. The back legs push hard against the ground and then straighten out, throwing the frog forward. The action is a little like releasing a coiled spring. All animals that use their back limbs to jump have very strong muscles.

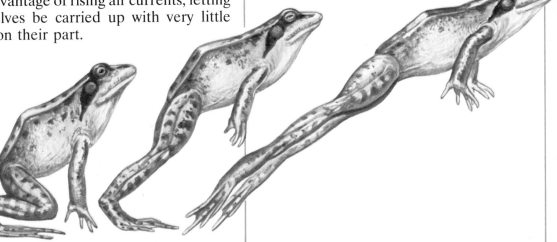

THE FASTEST ANIMALS

tench 1-1/4 mph

tuna 13-1/2 mph

pike 15-1/2 mph

shark 22 mph

whale 31 mph

swordfish 60 mph

sailfish 68 mph

Which are the fastest fish?
The diagram, left, shows the fastest speeds of different fish. The sailfish is the fastest, reaching speeds of sixty-eight miles per hour. If you watch a fish swim you can see that it begins by moving its tail, from left to right and vice versa, while maintaining its fin vertical to its body. The tail fin can be considered like the blade of a propeller that moves from side to side instead of revolving. The other fins stabilize the fish in the water or aid in limited movements.

Which are the fastest land animals?
The fastest is surely the cheetah, but the gazelle is also a very impressive runner. The ostrich can reach speeds of up to fifty miles per hour while the fastest speed that man can achieve is twenty-five miles per hour.

What are the fastest flying animals?

There are many animals that fly very fast including: huge numbers of insects, birds and, among mammals, the bat. Flying is the quickest means of travel and can carry an animal the farthest. A chimney swift can fly at up to two hundred seventeen miles per hour which is the record for speed in the animal kingdom, even though the frigate bird, right, dives at almost two hundred fify miles per hour.

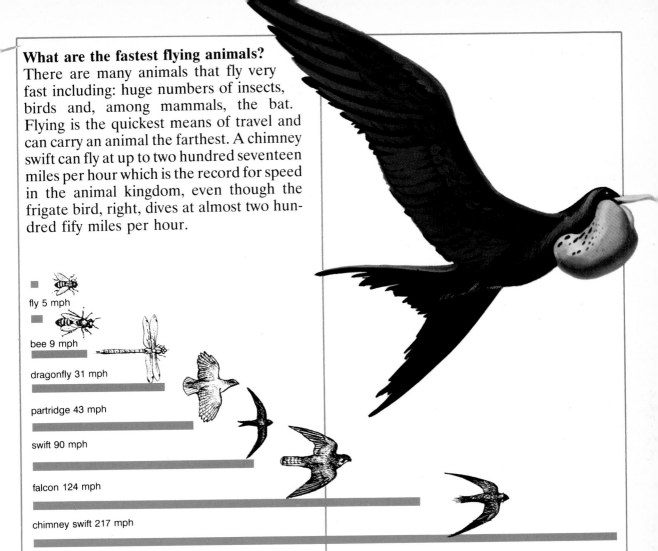

fly 5 mph

bee 9 mph

dragonfly 31 mph

partridge 43 mph

swift 90 mph

falcon 124 mph

chimney swift 217 mph

Is it true that the cheetah can run faster than seventy-five miles per hour?

Yes. The speed record for the cheetah, a member of the cat family living in the African savannah, is well over seventy-five miles per hour.

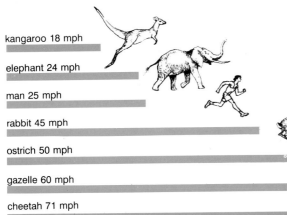

kangaroo 18 mph

elephant 24 mph

man 25 mph

rabbit 45 mph

ostrich 50 mph

gazelle 60 mph

cheetah 71 mph

Are there any animals that do not move at all?

There are aquatic animals like the sea anemone and corals that do not move. They live firmly attached to the bottom of the sea. But even they must sometimes move parts of their bodies to defend themselves and to get food. The white polyps of the coral for example have a crown of tentacles that surround their mouth and can move or be retracted.

THE PREDATORS

What is a predator?

A predator is an animal that attacks and kills other animals for food. All of the animal world is organized into a kind of food chain, in which animals prey on other animals and are in turn preyed upon themselves.

The chain is dominated by a relatively small number of large predators who must work hard to catch their prey.

Among mammals, the majority of predators are carnivores, including tigers, lions, foxes, wolves and many others. They display a wide variety of adaptation and specialization in their methods of attack, both in their appearance and in their behavior.

Is the pike a predator?

Yes, the pike is considered the most fearsome of all the freshwater fish in Europe. At left you can see a pike about to capture a tench.

However, the tench, though a victim of the pike, is also a predator itself. It feeds on small crustaceans.

Is the marten the most agile predator?

In the forests of Europe there are several medium-sized and small predators including the weasel, marten and pole cat, that can capture their prey with strikes of lightning speed. The marten (above left, pursuing a squirrel), is the most agile of the preying mammals.

What kind of specialization is there among predators?

There are many kinds. Some animals, like the cats, are adapted to run very fast and make sudden pounces, moving very silently, and catching their victim by surprise. Others, such as the canines, like wolves, jackals and wild dogs, hunt in packs and follow their prey, shifting directions and attacking their victim as a group once they catch it.

Bears, use their big paws to fish for salmon in the summer when these fish swim upstream to deposit their eggs.

The marine otter is a specialist in shellfish. Lying on its back, belly-up in the water, it holds a rock with its hind paws and crushes mollusks against it with its front paws.

Is the bear the largest predator of the arctic regions?

The polar bear lives mainly on seals and small walruses, but he himself is sometimes the prey of the killer whale, which is probably the largest and most voracious of the predatory animals. The remains of thirteen penguins and fourteen seals were once found in a killer whale's stomach.

Do lions hunt in packs?

Yes, lions are the only felines that practice a kind of collective hunt. But unlike canines, like the wolf, they do not pursue their prey over long distances.

NATURE'S CLEANERS

What are nature's cleaners?
There are many animals whose main job is to keep their surroundings clean. They get rid of the carcasses of dead animals and natural waste that would otherwise become serious pollutants.
Because of their work, they are called nature's cleaners.

What kinds of animals are "cleaners"?
The best known of those that eat carrion, are birds like the vulture and condor and animals like the jackal and hyena.
But no less important is the work of the "cleaner" insects, like the dung beetle (pictured above right), who lives on the waste of other animals. Bacteria and other microorganisms take care of the final breakdown of organic material.

How does the cleaning process work?
Let us imagine that a predatory animal like the lion attacks and kills a zebra. After it has finished eating the most appetizing parts, it abandons the carcass. Then vultures, with their keen eyesight, spot the remains. They circle over it and then swoop down on the carcass, and with their sharp curved beaks pick off the scraps still stuck to the bones. At the same time, bands of jackals and hyenas draw near and eat the rest. Finally nothing remains of the zebra but a very clean skeleton. Over time it will begin to flake and crumble, called bacterial decomposition, and become an excellent food for the soil.

What is the nitrogen cycle?
When animals die, their remains eventually decompose and help fertilize the soil by releasing nitrogen into it. Plants which grow in this soil are eaten by animals, which in turn, eat other animals. Eventually they die and the cycle starts again.

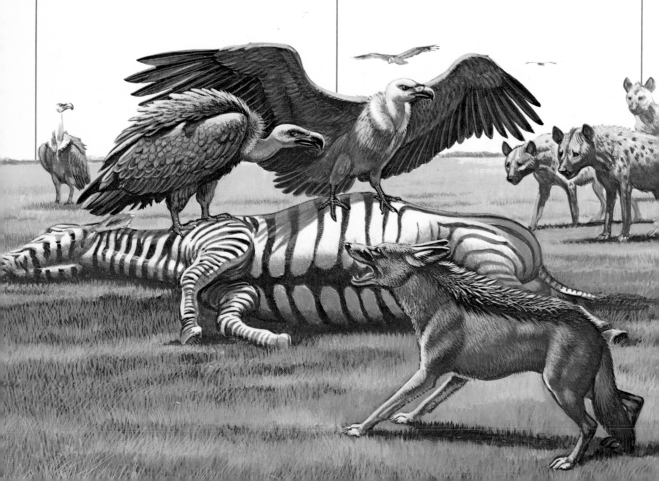

What do dung beetles do?
Their name defines their job. These insects collect animal dung to use as a reserve food supply by making tiny balls that they pull along until they find a place to bury them. Very often, they also use these balls of dung as places to deposit their eggs.

And what do "burying" beetles do?
Unlike the dung beetle, the food of these insects comes from small carrion, like mice, voles and small birds that the large predators are not interested in.

To take possession of the dead animal, the beetles work as a group. Once they have spotted a carcass, they begin to dig around it, removing the soil under it until they have made a hole in which they can bury the small animal. It will then become an important source of food for the adult beetles and their larva.

Are flies ever useful?
We know that, especially in summer, we must cover up food to keep flies away, because of the harmful bacteria they deposit. But sometimes they render a valuable service to nature. They often lay their eggs on a carcass. When the larva are born, they are very hungry and will devour the carcass, thus helping in the breakdown of an organism and the return to the soil of inorganic compost.

What other insects use the waste materials of animals?
The hornet does. It digs out tunnels under cow dung and after depositing its eggs there, fills the tunnels up with the waste material.

What has man learned from nature's cleaners?
We have seen that the demolition of plant and animal refuse by many insects is an important part of our natural environment. The fact that bacteria and microorganisms can reduce waste material to a harmless, even useful substance has been exploited by man to produce fertilizers that work on cultivated soil the same way, enriching it with nutritious substances. This allows important elements, especially nitrates, that would otherwise disappear, to be returned to the soil.

MIGRATION

Why do some animals migrate?

When the weather turns colder, many species of animals migrate to warmer climates. Wild geese and ducks make their nests in the Nordic countries and splash about happily in the cold water in the summer. But when the ponds freeze over they are no longer able to dive to the bottom to find food. When this happens they band together and fly south.

tern 11,200 miles

willow warbler 8,000 miles

plover 7,400 miles

swallow 5,500 miles

grey whale 5,000 miles

flamingo 3,700 miles

monarch butterfly 1,800 miles

How far do they go?

The chart above shows the distance that some migratory animals travel. The champion migrant is the stern. This bird, which spends its summers near the North Pole, flies across almost half the earth, stopping near the South Pole.

Do bison migrate?

Today bison live in the wild only in parts of Canada and in the national parks of America. But winter is a problem for them, too. When snow covers their pastures, they must move toward warmer lands in the south and the west in order to find food.

Is it true that the monarch butterfly flies over one thousand eight hundred miles?

Animals even smaller than birds are able to travel very long distances. One of them is the North American monarch butterfly. Every year it travels from Canada to Mexico, a distance of over one thousand eight-hundred miles. Its trip is a long one indeed, but what makes this insect even more extraordinary is that it makes the journey on paper-thin wings and it weighs less than one-tenth of an ounce.

Why does the salmon travel back upstream?

Salmon are born in large holes in freshwater streams where the mother has deposited her eggs. They live in these streams for about two years, then they head downstream toward the sea. After a few years, when the time has come to reproduce, instinct draws them back to the place where they were born. Only there will they deposit their eggs. This journey, from the sea upstream, may be thousands of miles long.

Are grasshoppers destructive?

Not all grasshoppers are destructive to crops, but locusts are. They are found throughout Asia and Africa where they form very hungry swarms of millions. If they cannot find food, especially during a drought, they migrate in search of new lands, bringing destruction as they go along, eating everything in their path, right down to the last blade of grass.

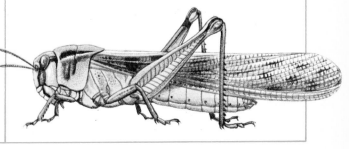

HIBERNATION

Why do animals sleep?

All animals, including man, need to sleep from time to time. This allows their bodies to replace the energy they use up during the day. When they sleep, their blood circulation slows down and their nervous system relaxes. Some animals extend this period of sleep for long periods at certain times of the year.

What is hibernation?

Hibernation is a physiological process in which vital functions stop almost completely. The body temperature drops sharply (the temperature of a marmot can fall to twenty five degrees Fahrenheit!), the heart beat slows down and the need for food is reduced to a minimum.

When do animals go into hibernation?

Hibernation is linked to survival in a hostile atmosphere. Therefore, the period of hibernation coincides with the onset of winter with its cold weather and abundant snowfalls, when the search for food becomes difficult.

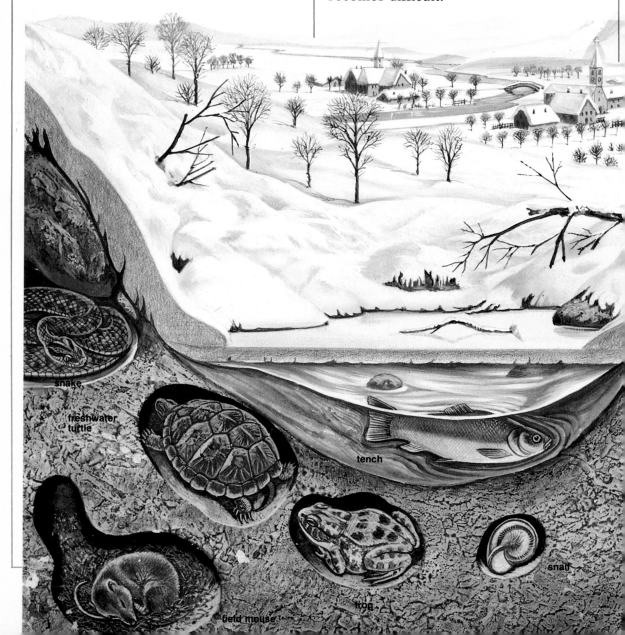

snake

freshwater turtle

tench

field mouse

frog

snail

Which animals hibernate?
Warm-blooded animals such as birds and mammals do, as well as some insects and reptiles. Among birds, the little hummingbird reaches a state near hibernation, called lethargy, which is not quite as deep as hibernation.

Where do they go when they hibernate?
They go underground or into holes in trees. The squirrel and the dormouse make lairs in a tree. Some insects, such as ants, hibernate under the bark of a tree. Marmots, small rodents, frogs and snakes burrow into the ground.

Do they stay asleep the whole time they are in hibernation?
This depends. Some animals wake up every so often to eat, drink and eliminate waste. Others do not move for months.

How long can they survive without food?
Squirrels increase their layer of fat noticeably in the summer so they will have a reserve for the winter when they hibernate. The hamster, on the other hand, keeps stores of food in its burrow.

Do animals hibernate only in the winter?
Yes, but in hot dry weather, a similar process called "estivation" takes place. Then, animals go into a state of torpidity, or sluggishness, to survive a period of heat when there is little food or moisture.

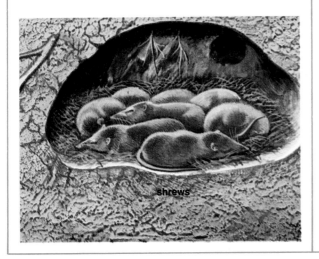

shrews

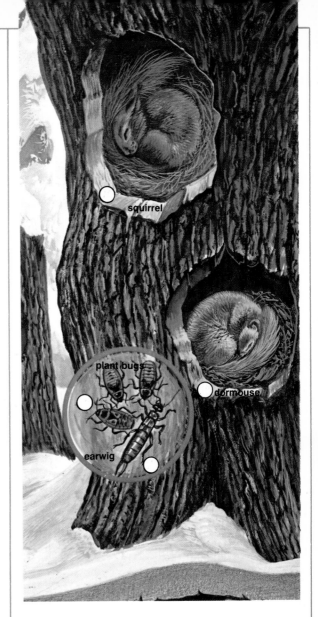

squirrel

plant bugs

dormouse

earwig

Are animals the only ones that hibernate?
Since hibernation is a time when the vegetative activities of an organism slow down or stop, plants also have a period of rest that coincides with winter hibernation.

When does hibernation end?
When spring arrives, animals may wake up from dormancy very quickly. Their body temperature, which had dropped very low during hibernation, can go up to eighty-six degrees in a matter of hours. The unexpected burst of energy that accompanies the rise wakes the animal up into a period of intense activity.

METAMORPHOSIS

Why does the outer appearance of some animals change?

While for most animals growth is a phenomenon that involves the whole body, an insect with a rigid body covering is forced to change its shell several times. This is because while its body grows, the covering does not. So, to grow a larger body, an insect must get rid of the older smaller shell first.

What is metamorphosis?

When we see a butterfly in the spring, what strikes us most is the beautiful colors of its wings. We pay little attention to its tiny body. And yet that small body has a long history. When the egg of the butterfly hatched, a little grub, or larva, appeared, usually brown or green and without any wings at all. Before it could look like its mother, the grub has to change its appearance, undergoing a complete transformation called "metamorphosis.".

How many stages must an insect go through to become an adult?

Once it has hatched, a grub goes through three basic stages, each with its own name: larva, pupa or chrysalis and adult. In the larva stage, the insect is quite hungry. Illustrated below are the three stages of a hawk-moth, from larva to chrysalis to adult.

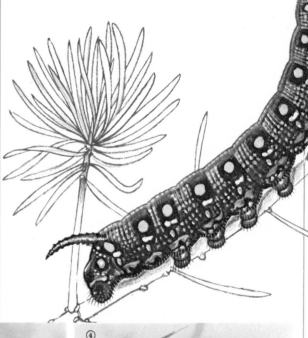

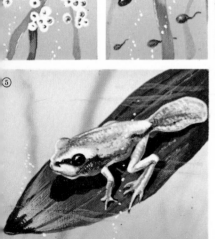

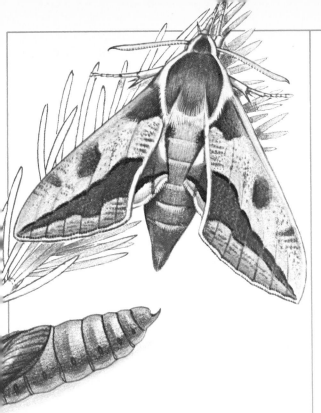

What is the chrysalis or pupa?

After a period of rapid growth, the larva lives for a time in a state of absolute immobility, eating nothing.

This is the most important moment in its life, because it is at this point that it is transforming itself into an adult.

Are insects the only animals that undergo a metamorphosis?

No, there are other examples among amphibians, fish and crustaceans that also metamorphose.

In a metamorphosis, is it only the outside of the animal that changes?

Among amphibians, there is one example of a total change. The frog goes from a life that is aquatic to one that is terrestial (opposite page below). From an egg (1), a tadpole hatches (2) which resembles a tiny fish: it breathes through gills. As the tadpole grows, its gills become smaller until only the internal parts remain (3). Back legs develop (4), then forelegs (5), the tail disappears and the frog climbs out of the water (6). By now it has developed lungs and is an adult frog (7) who will spend the rest of his life both on land and in the water.

Why do amphibians go through such changes?

These animals are carry-overs from an important stage in the evolution of our planet: the transition of living things from life in the water to life on land. Their development reflects this great change.

Do metamorphoses happen in sea animals?

Yes, there are also cases of metamorphosis here. For example, when the sole hatches, it looks much like other fish, with one eye on each side of its body. As it grows, its body develops its characteristic flat shape and its two eyes move to the same side.

How long do such metamorphoses take?

The time need for an insect to change from a larva to an adult varies widely, depending on what kind of animal it is. From grub to butterfly, for example, may be a matter of only three to four weeks. The may bug (below) spends three, sometimes four years as a larva, during which time it lives on the ground, eating the young roots of plants.

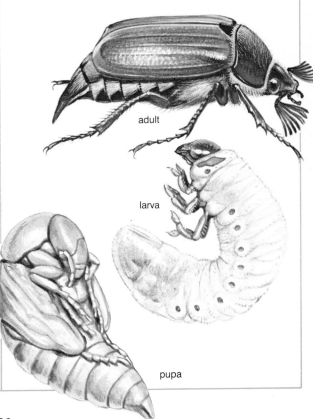

adult

larva

pupa

HOW ANIMALS CARE FOR THEIR YOUNG

Do animals "educate" their young?
Yes, birds, for example, teach their young many things, from how to fly to how to find food. But only among mammals is there a true kind of education. In humans, the teaching process becomes very complicated. Generally, the longer it takes for an animal to reach adulthood, the more care it requires from its parents.

How long do parents usually care for their babies?
This varies widely. Among birds, several weeks is all that is needed. But among mammals, the chamois, a goat-like antelope, will remain by its mother's side for a year, a lion cub for three years and a chimpanzee will be dependent on its mother for four to five years.

Why do they care for their young?
This care is closely linked to survival of the species in the animal world. Over the course of thousands of years, natural selection has forced animals to condition their behavior to this end.

How do parents teach their children?
Children are taught through sounds and touch. Among monkeys for example, the mother often caresses and holds her baby close to her to give it a feeling of security.

How do reptiles behave?
Most of the time there is very little interaction between mother and child reptiles, except for the ferocious crocodile. As soon as the eggs hatch, the mother takes the babies in her jaw and carries them to water.

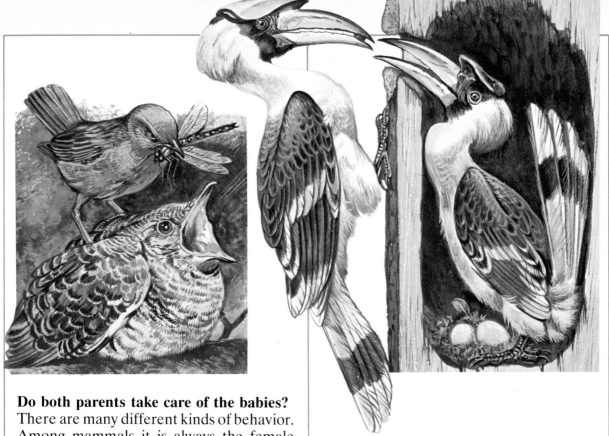

Do both parents take care of the babies?

There are many different kinds of behavior. Among mammals it is always the female who takes care of the young, feeding them and taking them on their first hunts. But among birds, there is close cooperation between both parents. Swallows, for example, feed their babies jointly and teach them to fly. With other birds, the mother sits on the nest and the father gets the food. The male Great Indian Hornhill, above right, walls up the female in the hole of a tree to protect her and their young. He brings food to the family and passes it through a small opening.

Are there any "bad" parents in the animal kingdom?

There are a few among birds. The European cuckoo, for example, takes no interest in its young at all. In fact, it leaves its eggs in the nests of other birds. The other birds become adoptive parents and care for the young, not even realizing the offspring are not their own. The young cuckoo will be equally "bad." As it grows up, it will not hesitate to drive the young of its new parents out of the nest (above left).

Are there any unusual mothers?

The most unusual mother must be the opossum which lives in North America. A few days after the young are born, the mother opossum puts her young on her back and does not leave them for a moment. With their own tails, the babies hold on to her strong tail, which is as stiff as the branch of a tree.

SOCIABLE ANIMALS

Does a group spirit exist among animals?
The survival of many species of animals depends on their ability to form groups. Collective life, in fact, guarantees the adults protection for themselves and, by careful protection of the young, the continuity of the species.

What is the basis for a society?
Among mammals, the starting point is the family, while among insects, the society is based on a careful division of labor. In the first case, the family is necessary for the care of the young. In the second, it is the number of individuals cooperating on a range of activities that makes survival possible.

Are there any solitary animals?
Yes. For example, the praying mantis is such an aggressive insect that it will not tolerate others of its kind near it.

How do elephants take care of each other?
The closest ties among these animals are between mother and children. After an almost two-year period of gestation (carrying the unborn baby in the mother's womb), young elephants need to be cared for and protected for a long time. When they are on the march or resting, the herd is careful to surround the young, with the mothers staying next to their babies. The males walk ahead and lead the herd. In case of danger, the males sound the alarm, but it is mainly the females who will defend the little ones.

Do penguins protect each other?
Both the male and the female penguin sit on the eggs. When they hatch, all of the baby penguins are brought into penguin society together and cared for jointly by everyone, regardless of who the original parents are. Penguins are rather defenseless creatures, and if the parents are killed, this means that the young will still be cared for. Penguins can form colonies of thousands.

Why do monkeys pick lice off each other?

The drawing below shows some Macaque monkeys busy with a well-known activity, "delousing."

Besides its hygenic use to eliminate parasites, delousing is a symbol of social standing in the monkey community.

Individuals of lesser importance occupy themselves with the grooming of those of greater importance.

In the illustration, the most important monkey is the one the far left. Standing diminishes until you reach the last monkey on the right. Even babies learn the iron-clad laws of hierarchy early on.

Which insects live in groups?

Ants, bees, and termites are the most organized insects, with distinct social classes according to their jobs.

There are the workers, who look for food and nourishment for the queen, the soldiers, who defend the group, and the queen, who is responsible for their reproduction.

Which is the oldest society among insects?

The termite, without any doubt has the oldest society. But in this case, "oldest" does not mean primitive or particularly simple. One need only think of the complexity of their colonies, real cities complete with labyrinths created in tropical regions. Their mounds can reach heights of more than fifteen feet above the ground. While ant hills swarm with workers coming and going, in termite nests you will not see any termites above the ground. The access tunnels and chambers are generally below ground, hidden in the roots of a tree or under rocks. Like bees and ants, termite reproduction is dependent on the queen who is attended to and fed by young termites. Shortly before depositing her eggs, she becomes gigantic in relation to the other termites (see above).

SYMBIOSIS AND MUTUALISM

What is symbiosis?

In biology symbiosis is the interdependence of two or more organisms of different species upon each other. The species that form this relationship always live together and get certain things from the relationship that they need for their survival. Mutualism is another association from which species get certain things. But in mutualism, the two organisms are not forced to live together because each one is able to live independently of the other.

How does the hermit crab behave?

The hermit crab is a shellfish that, to protect its soft abdomen from predators, crawls into an abandoned shell. A sea anemone then attaches itself to the shell. The crab moves the shell about taking the sea anemone with it, making the sea anemone search for food easier. In return, the sea anemone defends the crab from predators with its tentacles.

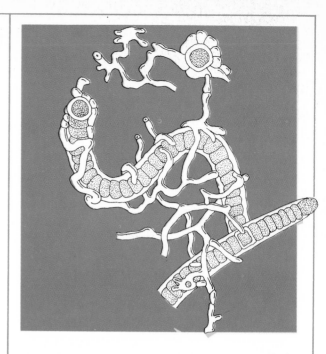

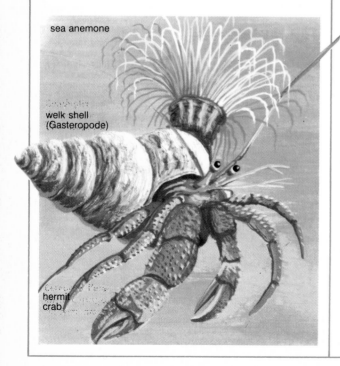

sea anemone

welk shell
(Gasteropode)

hermit
crab

Are there cases of symbiosis in the plant world?

Many fungi, for example, form relationships with other plants, giving them some of the water absorbed by their spawn, the cells that form the mycelium of the fungi. The hosts of the fungus, in return, give them some of the food they manufacture. This kind of symbiosis is called mycorrhiza. The best known example is the relationship between fungus and algae. The product of this close association is a particular type of plant organism, the lichen, able to live and prosper even in the most inhospitable regions, like the arctic.

Who "brushes" the crocodile's teeth?

What kind of animal would dare enter the mouth of a crocodile? Yet there is one little bird, called the "crocodile bird," that is just that brave. The crocodile lets it wander freely in its mouth to pick its teeth for food. In return, the bird gets rid of parasites, especially leeches, from the gums of the reptile.

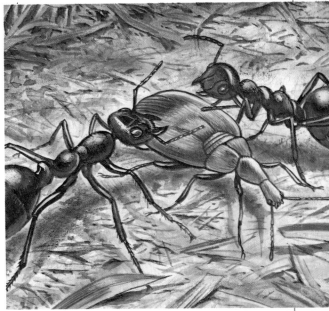

Who does the tuatara live with?

The tuatara is a strange reptile that lives on the New Zealand island of Karewa. On the same tiny island lives the puffin. Since there is very little space on the island, the two animals have learned how to live together. The puffin takes care of the building of a nest and the tuatara, a formidable consumer of insects, keeps it clean. In this way, the bird and the reptile live together as good friends.

Why do ants "raise" certain insects?

In an ant hill, there often live other insects besides the ant, in particular, the aphid. Instead of being attacked, these insects are cared for and nourished by the ants. Of course this behavior is not altruistic (without personal gain). The aphids have special glands that produce a sugary substance called honeydew which the ants like very much. Therefore, each benefits from the other.

ANIMAL BEHAVIOR

Is animal behavior due to instinct?
In general, animals behave instinctively but in some cases they learn by imitation or from experience.

How do they learn?
The most significant example of learning from experience is that of the chimpanzee. When a bunch of bananas is placed out of the animal's reach, it will try all sorts of ways to get it.
After several unsuccessful attempts, it will take a stick and some object on which to climb, so it can reach the fruit.

Do animals comunicate with each other?
Each species has its own language. It can be expressed with sounds, odors or visual signals. Among the last, the best known example is the language of the fivefly.

When do fireflies exchange signals?
During the period of courtship, the male firefly, giving off a continuous light with his abdomen, flies over a meadow, hoping to find a female. When the female, who is wingless, sees the signal, she responds with a flashing light.

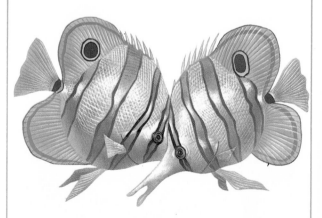

Does aggression exist in the animal world?
Yes, aggressive behavior can be found in the animal world, especially among males fighting to win a female. In the fish world, for example, the delicate butterfly fish do a kind of "arm wrestling," by pushing their heads against each other.

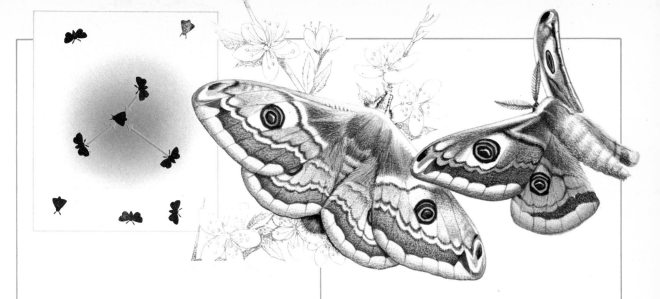

How do insects communicate?

Among insects, the most common language used is that of odor. The scented aura around a female butterfly is meant to attract males, who can find her several yards away. The ant leaves a scented trail over the ground which, if destroyed, makes it hard for the ant to find its way home. When a cockroach finds food, it gives off an odor to attract its friends. In this case, the signal is called a "recruiting" signal. The insects perceive these odorous signals with their sensitive antennas.

Do animals use any particular devices to get their food?

There are many case of ingenuity and cleverness in this sense among animals. For example, the oyster catcher feeds on mussels and other mollusks. Using its sharp beak like a chisel, it forces it into the soft tasty contents of the shell. It can also open the shell by cracking it on a sharp stone or use its beak like a wedge to open the shells. Among insects, the larva of the lion ant wait hidden in their hole until some insect falls in. Then they stun it with a toxic paralyzing liquid and suck out its vital fluids.

BIRDS

What are the characteristics of birds?

Birds are vertebrates that have wings and a body covered with quills and feathers. They are oviparous, reproducing with eggs and have lungs and a circulatory system similar to man's. Descendants of reptiles, they appeared on earth more than one hundred forty million years ago. The first known bird fossil is the "Archaeopterys," whose remains are in the Natural History Museum in London. Birds come in great variety, and can be divided into more than nine thousand different species. Some birds stay in one place and never leave it while others are migratory, traveling incredible distances to find better climates.

Where do birds live and what do they eat?

There are birds all over the earth, from the polar regions to the equator, in rivers, lakes and streams and the highest mountain peaks. They eat a wide variety of plants, animals and insects according to their species and the climatic conditions.

What are their beaks for and why are there so many different shapes?

Instead of mouths, birds have beaks, with no teeth, which they use to peck at plants and poke into the earth, searching for food. The beak is also used to feed their young, to clean and comb their feathers and to build a nest. The shape of the beak has evolved in different species to help them as they hunt for food. There are long slender beaks like that of the hummingbird in the illustration, beaks like pliers, flat beaks and hooked beaks. Scientists studying the shape of beaks and the way they are used have likened them to tools used by man.

How do birds fly?

The bones of birds are a bit like inner tubes: they are hollow and connected to air sacks throughout the body. This means that the bird is lightweight, making it easier to fly. The propulsive force of flight comes from the wings which are attached to a bony ridge jutting out from the breastbone, called the keel, or carina.

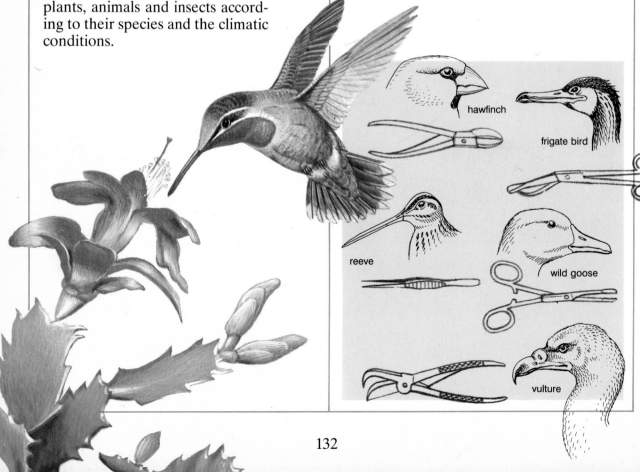

hawfinch

frigate bird

reeve

wild goose

vulture

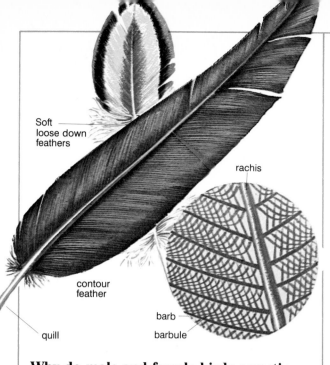

Soft loose down feathers

rachis

contour feather

barb

barbule

quill

What are feathers used for?

The feathers protect the body of a bird from the cold. This is important because birds are warm-blooded animals.

Feathers are also indispensable for flight. The feathers consists of a reed-like part called a quill attached to a small sac of skin and another part connected to the shaft that consists of branch-like barbs with tiny hooked "whiskers" called barbules growing from them (see illustration, left). Feathers are lightweight and waterproof and come in all kinds of patterns and colors.

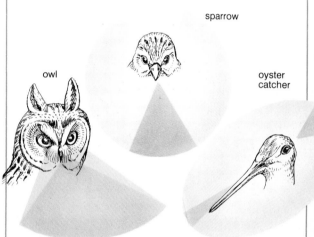

sparrow

owl

oyster catcher

Why do male and female birds sometimes have completely different colors?

Sometimes the male of a species has very different colored or shaped plumage from the female. This is called "sexual dimorphism" and it often plays a role in attracting a mate during courtship. The best known birds with this characteristic are the peacock, the duck and the pheasant. An example of a male and female pheasant is shown below.

How do birds see?

Birds have very keen eyesight because of the way their eyes are placed in their heads. In the drawing above, the darkest color indicates the binocular field of vision (i.e., using both eyes) of three birds. As you can see, the oyster catcher can see all the way behind him, giving him a range of three hundred sixty degrees.

LIFE IN LAKES AND PONDS

Do many organisms live in lakes and ponds?
Yes, lakes and ponds are places where many special forms of life prosper. You can see some of them portrayed below. If you could look at a drop of water taken from a lake or pond under a microscope, you would see an even more interesting sight (below left): among the filaments of microscopic green algae swim tiny protozoa and minute worms. Every so often a "big" crustacean makes its appearance. Measuring a fraction of an inch, it can be seen with the naked eye.

Is there much microscopic plant life in this environment?
Yes, there is. The green algae we mentioned is one example. There are also diatrom, many different kinds of flagellated algae like the green algae, with some types able to move as fast as many protozoa, and the elegant Ceratium with its long horn-shaped body. All of these microscopic plants are known as plant plankton.

What does a kingfisher eat?
The kingfisher is a brightly colored bird with a long strong beak, a large head, and short lopped-off wings and tail. Perched on a branch, it may spend hours scrutinizing the surface of the water in a pond. When it sees a fish, it dives down headfirst and emerges with its prey in its beak.

water lily

dragonfly

mallard duck

green frog

aquatic ranunculus

stickleback

limnaea

newt

Why do water lilies float?

The leaves and flowers of the water lily float because they are filled with air pockets that work a little like rubber rafts. They are in close contact with the submerged parts of the plant, guaranteeing them the necessary oxygen and carbon dioxide.

What is special about the water chestnut?

The water chestnut with a Latin name of "Trapa natans," is an annual that grows frequently in marshy places and along the banks of lakes and streams. Its seeds have strong rigid hooks that anchor it to the muddy bottom of ponds and streams where it germinates. Its fruit is edible.

cattails

kingfisher

arrowhead

otter

seaweed

chub

water snail

freshwater sponge

water bug

carp

CETACEA, THE SEA MAMMALS

Are Cetacea fish?
No, Cetacea, such as whales, dolphins and the porpoise, are mammals just like dogs, cows and man. Their bodies have changed over time to make them perfectly adapted to aquatic life. Instead of gills, they have huge lungs that allow them to stay under water for long periods. They have one or two nostrils, or spouts, from which they emit a watery spray.

Where do they live?
In general, they live in salt water, except for some species that are found in freshwater rivers and lakes, such as the Ganges River Dolphin.

humpback whale

bowhead whale

grey California whale

When did they appear on earth?
According to fossil studies, Cetacea appeared about fifty million years ago.

How many sub-orders of Cetacea exist?
Cetacea are divided into Odontoceti and Mysticeti. Odontoceti have between two and two hundred fifty teeth, one nostril and are carnivores. There are about seventy species of Odontoceti, among them the dolphin, the porpoise, the killer whale, the narwhal and sperm whales. The Mysticeti have no teeth. Instead they have a series of thin horny plates hanging down in their mouth, almost like fringes, called baleen. The baleen trap huge quantities of marine life called krill which they feed on. This group has two blowholes and includes the blue and humpback whales.

What are the main characteristics of Cetacea?
Cetacea have long streamlined bodies adapted to living in the water. Their hydrodynamic shape allows them to reach speeds up to forty miles per hour in short bursts. The neck is short and fixed; the skull varies depending on the species. The fins are used for navigation and stabilization, the fluke or paddle-like tail produces forward motion.

Do Cetacea live in groups?
Mysticeti live alone or in small groups while Odontoceti tend to live in loose groups of twenty to twenty-five or more. If one member of the group is ill or wounded the others will remain close by and try to help it.

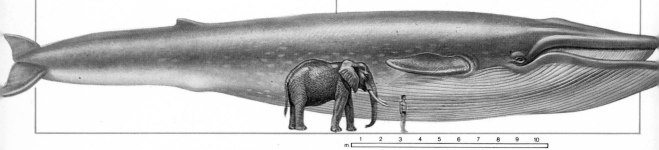

narwhal

How are the babies born?
Like all mammals, the young develop in the mother's womb. The babies are born in the water and are nursed. The relationship between mother and child is intense and lasts until the calf is weaned, at around eighteen months.

Do whales migrate?
Whales with baleen live in the polar regions but they move to more temperate waters to give birth. Each year they make long migrations of more than six thousand eight hundred miles round trip looking for food and a place to reproduce.

Which is the largest of the Cetacea?
The blue whale is not only the largest whale but the largest animal in the world. It measures up to one hundred five feet long and can weigh up to one hundred forty tons.

Where do sperm whales live?
Sperm whales live in both warm and temperate waters. They are carnivores and their favorite food is squid. The sperm whale's head contains a highly valued oily substance called spermaceti which is used to make candles and cosmetics. The sperm whale is the largest of the Odontoceti. Males grow as large as sixty feet long while females measure up to fifty feet.

How can you tell Cetacea apart from each other?
It is not very hard to recognize different species of Cetacea. You only need to pay attention to a few things, as you can see in the chart on the left.
Among the characteristics of this species are the size and shape of the spray of water expelled when the animals surface. Another characteristic is the shape of the dorsal fin that sticks up as the animal goes under. Some whales have no dorsal fins at all while others, like the blue whale, do. Below is one that does, the killer whale. This animal, like the dolphin, takes huge leaps out of the water.

sperm whale

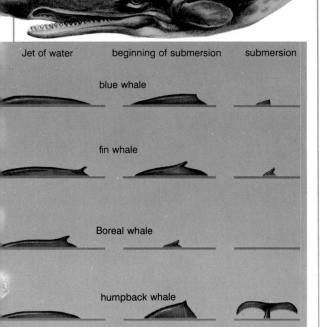

Jet of water | beginning of submersion | submersion

blue whale

fin whale

Boreal whale

humpback whale

gray California whale

bowhead whale

sperm whale

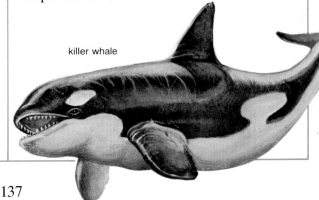

killer whale

137

ENDANGERED SPECIES

California condor

Cuban solenodon

Galapagos cormorant

When is an animal considered to be an endangered species?

A species is considered endangered when its population is drastically reduced so that it is in danger of extinction.

What are the causes of extinction?

Before man's appearance on earth, extinction was largely due to a process of natural selection where only those species able to adapt to a changing world survive while others, the weaker, die, as happened to the dinosaur. According to studies based on fossil remains, a species of animal became extinct every thousand years. But since the beginning of this century and the spread of technology, which is constantly reducing the amount of space for natural habitats, the rate of extinction has grown at a frightening pace. It is now at about one species a year.

Besides destroying natural habitats, man has also upset the balance of nature by hunting, often for sport, and by the introduction of antagonistic species into the same environment. Man has also damaged natural habitats by destroying forests to obtain wood, mining the subsoil carelessly to obtain minerals, polluting the waters with industrial waste and using excessive amounts of pesticides to protect crops.

Can insecticides and polluted water cause a species to become extinct?

They certainly can. We can take as an example the peregrine falcon that has come very close to extinction. Its customary prey was ducks. These ducks ate fish and algae that grew in areas polluted with the chemical DDT. This insecticide accumulated in the bodies of the ducks and when the falcon ate them, the chemicals affected the amount of calcium the falcons produced in their eggs. In some cases the concentration of calcium in the shells was so low that the eggs broke before the young could hatch. In others the amount of calcium was so high that the babies were not able to break out of their shells.

blue whale

giant
panda

mountain
gorilla

wallaby

Which species are endangered?

The drawing above shows some of the best known species in danger. Other animals at risk because of man are the tortoise, hunted for its shell, the elephant, hunted for its ivory tusks, the crocodile, the wolf and large felines, hunted for their skins, and the whale, hunted for its baleen and oil.

How can we protect endangered species?

Plants and animals help to maintain the ecological balance needed for the survival of man. There are laws to protect animals in the wild and also those kept in national parks and zoos. These laws help protect certain animals from the danger of extinction. For some species a zoo is the only guarantee that it will be saved from a constantly more dangerous environment. Sometimes protecting a species is very complicated. This is the case with the bear, which can only survive if each individual has fifteen to thirty square miles of forest. For the survival of many groups of bears there must be large tracts of forest land.

DID YOU KNOW...?

What is the biggest bird in the world?
The ostrich is the largest. It is around eight feet tall and can weigh from one-hundred-ten to one-hundred-sixty-five pounds.

Why do some flowers open during the day and some at night?
It is a matter of the insects that fertilize them. Most flowers are fertilized by insects which are alert during the day, but a few are fertilized by night insects.

Where does the spitting cobra live?
It lives in South Africa. It was given that name because it can spit its poison and hit its prey from as far as six feet away.

Are there such things as giant butterflies?
In the American tropics there are some very large butterflies. "Attacus Atlas," a nocturnal butterfly, has a wingspan of almost ten inches.

How long does an ant live?
A worker ant lives from three to six years while the queen lives up to eighteen years!

Which is the longest snake?
It is the reticulated python which lives in Southeast Asia. The longest one measured so far was thirty three feet.

Do all vampire bats live on blood?
Most vampires are insectivores. Only three species feed exclusively on blood: the true vampires, Desmodus, Diaemus and Diphylla, found in the American tropics in Central America, the Amazon, Brazil and Mexico.

How do skunks defend themselves?
Skunks have glands situated near their anus that secrete a very unpleasant-smelling liquid. When a skunk is in danger, it turns its back on the intruder, lifts its tail and sprays the enemy with a very offensive irritating jet of this liquid. It can reach a target more than ten feet away.

What is mimicry?
It is the ability that some animals have to blend in with their background to confuse the enemy and protect themselves from danger.

What is an onager?
It is a member of the equine or horse family that lives in the Asian desert that is related to the wild ass.

What is a papaya?
It is a melon-like fruit that comes from a tree in the tropics with a round or elongated shape.

What does a queen bee eat?
She is nourished by royal jelly, a substance secreted from the glands in the head of the worker bee which contains sugar, protein and vitamins.

What is parasitism?
It is the association of two living things (plants or animals) in which one of them, the parasite, lives off the other, the host.

How did pilot fish get their names?
They were given this name because they swim in front of sharks and other fish and appear to guide them.

What is a plantigrade?
It is the name given to a mammal, like the bear or man, that walks on the whole sole of its foot.

How does the spider keep from getting stuck in its own web?
There are two kinds of threads in a spider's web. One is sticky and the other is dry. The spider knows which is which and stays on the dry threads.

What is sargassum?
It is a kind of brown algae typical of tropical and temperate seas. The largest mass of floating sargassum is in the Sargasso Sea which lies between the West Indies and the Azores in the Atlantic.

SCIENCE AND TECHNOLOGY

THE BIGGEST AIRPLANE IN THE WORLD

What is the biggest airplane in the world?

The world's largest airplane is the Boeing 747, also called the jumbo jet, shown below. It is nearly 230 feet long and 62 feet high, weighs 356 tons, has four engines, eighteen wheels and can carry up to 500 passengers.

How fast can it fly?

The Boeing 747 can reach a speed of 600 miles per hour at an altitude of 43,000 feet. In order to take off it needs a runway nearly two miles in length.

When was the first 747 built?

The first jumbo jet was built in the 1960s. The first flight of a 747 took place in 1969.

1 radar antenna (not visible in illustration)
2 first pilot
3 second pilot
4 flight engineer
5 stairway to flight deck and lounge
6 first class cabin
7 flight attendant
8 front undercarriage
9 snack bar
10 lavatory
11 upper lounge
12 gas cylinder storage
13 first class section
14 very high frequency antennae
15 engines
16 inner leading-edge slats
17 very high frequency satellite antenna
18 center leading-edge slats
19 outer leading-edge slats
20 radio antenna
21 outer flap
22 central flap
23 inner flap
24 wing structure (also acts as fuel tank)
25 galley

26 coach section
27 cargo storage
28 pressure bulkhead
29 tail of plane
30 de-icing mechanism
31-32 upper and lower rudders
33 nozzle of auxiliary turbine
34-35 elevators

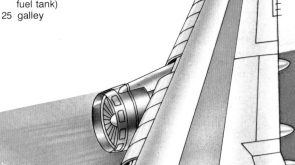

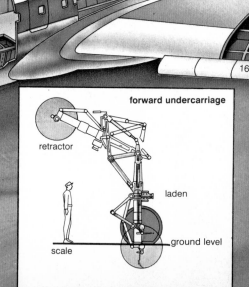

fire engine

ambulance

cargo loader

tow truck

boarding ramp

forward undercarriage

retractor

laden

scale

ground level

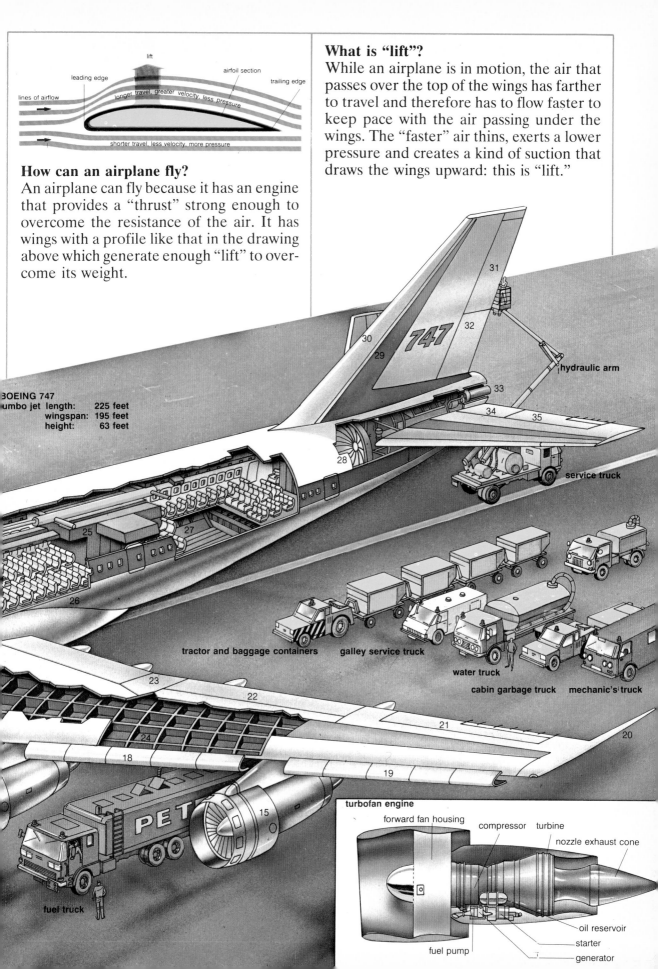

How can an airplane fly?

An airplane can fly because it has an engine that provides a "thrust" strong enough to overcome the resistance of the air. It has wings with a profile like that in the drawing above which generate enough "lift" to overcome its weight.

What is "lift"?

While an airplane is in motion, the air that passes over the top of the wings has farther to travel and therefore has to flow faster to keep pace with the air passing under the wings. The "faster" air thins, exerts a lower pressure and creates a kind of suction that draws the wings upward: this is "lift."

lift

leading edge

airfoil section

trailing edge

lines of airflow

longer travel, greater velocity, less pressure

shorter travel, less velocity, more pressure

747

30
29
31
32
33
34
35
28

hydraulic arm

service truck

BOEING 747
Jumbo jet length: 225 feet
wingspan: 195 feet
height: 63 feet

25
27
26
23
22
24
21
20
18
19
15

tractor and baggage containers

galley service truck

water truck

cabin garbage truck

mechanic's truck

fuel truck

turbofan engine

forward fan housing

compressor turbine

nozzle exhaust cone

oil reservoir

starter

generator

fuel pump

LEVER

SIMPLE MACHINES

What is a lever?

One of the oldest and most useful machines invented by man is the lever. This is a rigid bar that, when placed on or against a fixed support, allows very great weights to be lifted. More recently, levers were invented which, through the use of mechanical force, were capable of lifting even greater weights. This is what we now call the balance, a scale that has plates suspended from each arm for weighing goods.

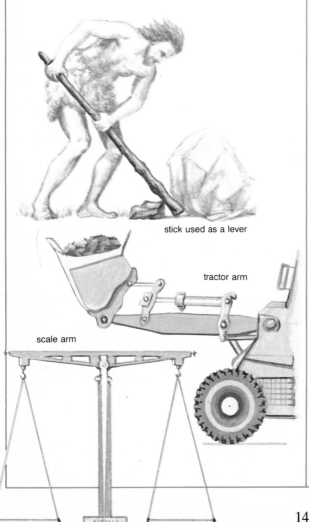

stick used as a lever

tractor arm

scale arm

WHEEL

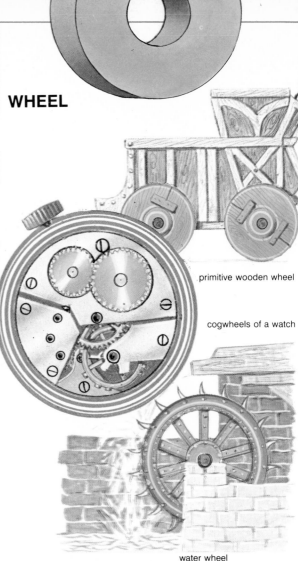

primitive wooden wheel

cogwheels of a watch

water wheel

Why is the wheel important?

The wheel is an invention that has transformed man's life. Wheels are used for many things, including: transportation, to form the gears that move machines, small instruments like watches and to use water from rivers as energy.

What are the wheel's main parts?

The wheel is shaped like a disk, turning around its own axis, and is made up of the hub, which connects the wheel to the axle, the rim, which is the outside part and may appear in different forms, and the spokes, which connect the rim to the hub. Depending on their use, wheels may or may not have "teeth." A "toothed" wheel is used for chains and pulleys, such as you would find on your bicycle

WEDGE
(sloping plane)

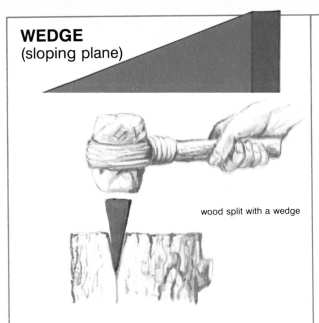

wood split with a wedge

What is the wedge and what are its uses?
The wedge is prism-shaped (triangular) with a sharply pointed front. Driven deep into an object (illustration above) it will split it or, in the case of the most widely-used wedge, the knife, cut it. Combined with other instruments it has very many uses: in a wood-plane it permits the smoothing of surfaces; as a point, attached to a jackhammer it will break very hard materials like rock; in a mechanical plow it makes deep breaking up of the ground possible.

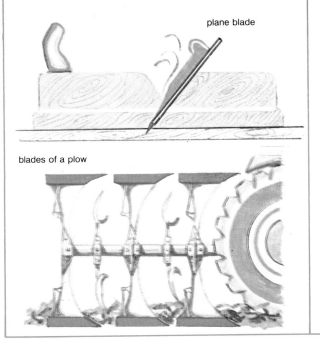

plane blade

blades of a plow

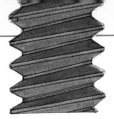

SCREWS

How are screws made?
Screws are basic mechanical elements that man finds many uses for. They are cylindrical or conical in form, and carry on part or all of their length a deep, helical incision called the "thread." They have two main parts, the shank and the head, but, depending on what they are being used for, have greatly differing sizes and threads. As drill bits they serve to make holes in wood and other materials. In a meat grinder they are used to force the meat against the cutting blade. Screws squeeze and compress when used in a press. The most common use of screws, however, is that of firmly fixing mechanical parts, or of joining different components.

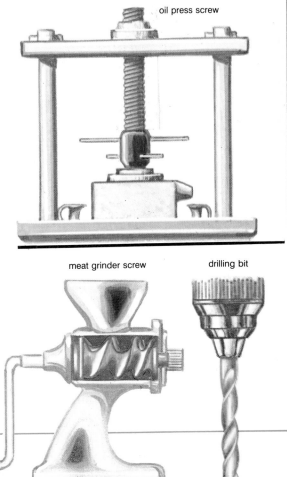

oil press screw

meat grinder screw

drilling bit

CINEMATOGRAPHY

When and how was the cinema (the moving picture) born?

When a light is waved in the dark, our eyes do not see the different points of light, but only one continuous line. By using a series of photographs in quick succession an impression of continuous movement is obtained. In 1895, Louis Lumière patented his cinematographic apparatus. It registered sixteen images per second and worked by a handle connected to a shutter that prevented the passage of light between one image and the next. The light rays were therefore intermittent, but because the images followed one another rapidly enough, the viewer received the impression of a moving picture.

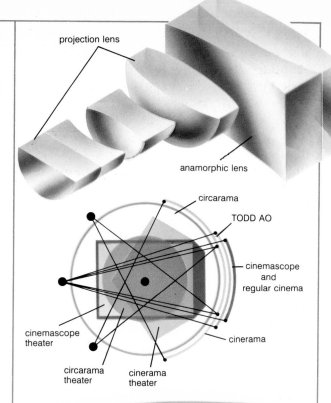

projection lens

anamorphic lens

circarama

TODD AO

cinemascope and regular cinema

cinerama

cinemascope theater

circarama theater

cinerama theater

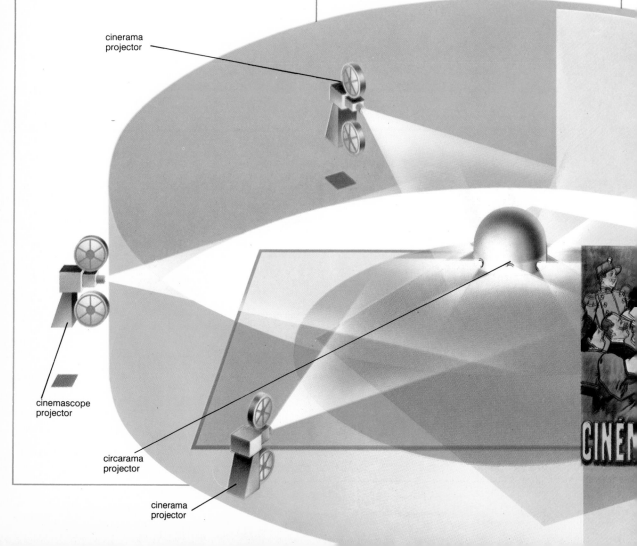

cinerama projector

cinemascope projector

circarama projector

cinerama projector

What new inventions exist today that incorporate the cinematographic technique?
Although the cinema is now largely superseded by televised broadcasting, it lives on still, due to certain innovations. Among these, some people relate to the sound effects provided by a movie theater that are impossible to obtain in the home, while others can appreciate the wide-angled projections. The anamorphic lens has allowed, within certain limits, the horizontal widening of the visual field. The anamorphic lens (see illustration at left) widens the angle of projection in cinemascope, while for even wider angles, several projectors may be used together. The drawing below shows the plan of the different projection rooms and of the angles of projection.

What are "cinerama" and "cinemascope"?
Most cinematographic progress comes from increasing the sense of realism and from giving the spectator the impression of being in another world, as happens in science fiction films, which incorporate a range of special effects. Cinerama, perfected in 1952, used three projectors and a curved screen to produce a more realistic angle of vision of seventy-eighty degrees (against the forty degrees of the normal screen) and simulated the peripheral outer edge vision of the eye. Cinerama also employed the use of several loudspeakers through which the soundtrack could be heard in all parts of the theater. By using cinemascope and panavision, a more recent development in the panoramic screen, the images projected are enlarged more horizontally than vertically, filling the angle of vision of the audience and giving a panorama wider than the eye can take in at a glance. The pictures below show three types of cinema screens.

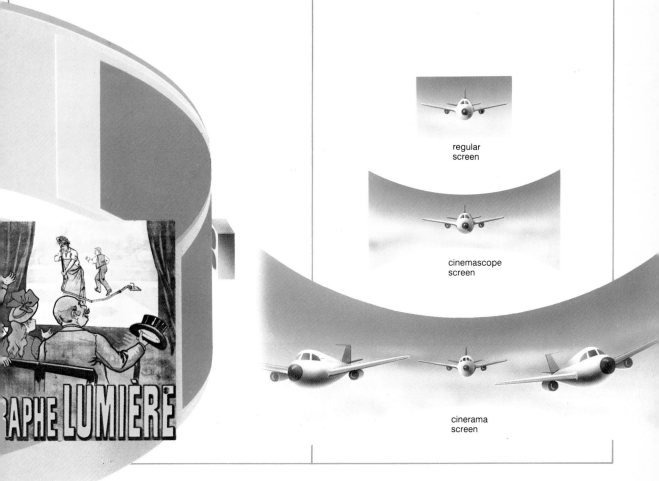

regular
screen

cinemascope
screen

cinerama
screen

APHE LUMIÈRE

PRINTING

What are today's printing techniques?
Three main kinds of printing exist today. They include: letterpress, rotogravure and offset.

What is the basic principle of printing?
The most complex techniques of printing are based on a simple procedure: the impressing onto paper of images or letters by means of stamps. The stamp, or matrix, carries either an embossed or incised letter, whole word, or a picture. Inked and pressed onto a page (see Fig. 1 below), the stamp leaves the imprint of the letter or the image. Alternatively, a cylinder on which the letter or image is raised or incised is inked and rolled onto a sheet of a paper, or the paper is made to run underneath the roller (see Fig. 2). In both cases a printed product is obtained.

How does letterpress printing work?
In letterpress printing the plate, made from letters in printer's metal, stands out. Because of this the ink covers only the outline of the letters and the page is produced by applying pressure onto paper.

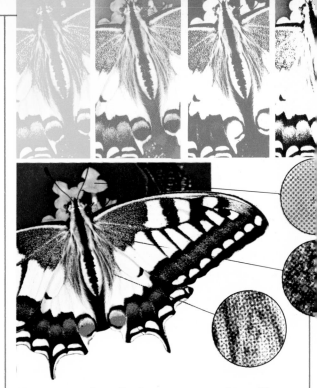

How are colored pictures reproduced?
Look at the butterfly above. You will see different colors, either "full" or in their various shades. This image is printed with four inks of different colors: yellow, red, blue and black. The first three are the primary colors; the black strengthens the three basic colors. The image to be reproduced is broken down into the basic colors, which are then superimposed on one another in four successive processes, reproducing the original image.

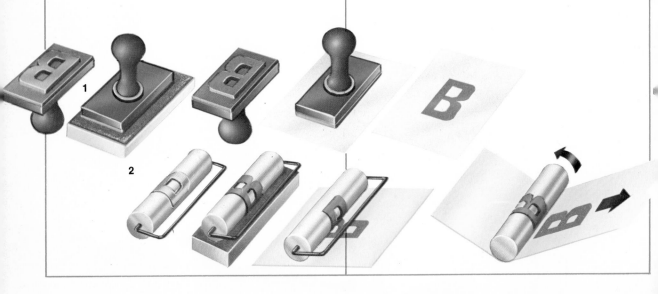

What is the screen?

If you look at a colored image through a magnifying glass you will see that it is composed of many little dots. It is these dots which can vary in size and in distance from one another, that make the different shades of color. The color is brighter when the dots are bigger (when the holes in the screen are wider), and paler when the dots are smaller.

Why do printing machines have four rollers?

Four basic colors exist when colors are broken down: yellow, red, blue and black. Each roller is then inked with one of these colors (see the illustration below). The paper runs under each roller, and when the colors have been exactly superimposed, the original image is obtained.

How does a rotogravure press work?

This is a system of printing with cylinders in which the letters and images are engraved or etched onto special plates. The ink fills all the grooves and a blade wipes off the excess. The paper, wrapped around a roller, is pressed against the inked plate which is also mounted on a roller. This is the way most newspapers are printed.

How does an offset press work?

This kind of printing uses neither relief nor engraving. It is done by means of plates sensitized with special acids. The ink sticks to the sensitized parts which are the parts to be printed while it slips off the others.

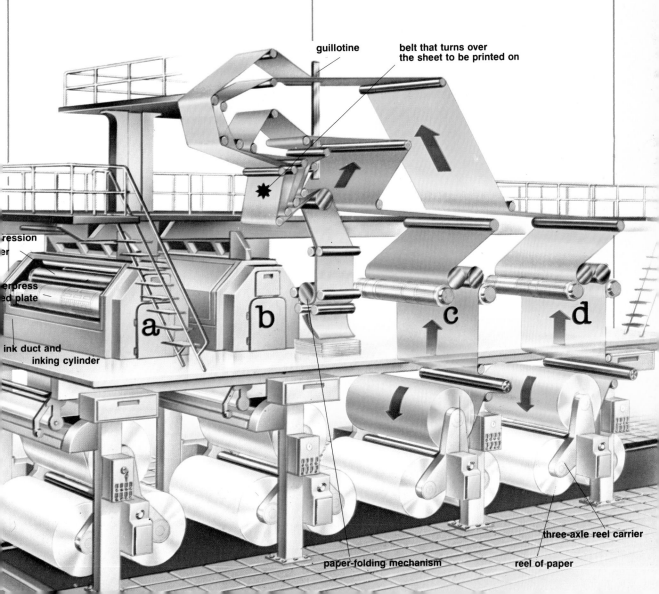

guillotine

belt that turns over the sheet to be printed on

ression
er

erpress
d plate

ink duct and inking cylinder

a

b

c

d

three-axle reel carrier

paper-folding mechanism

reel of paper

THE MODEL T FORD

Why is the Model T Ford important in the history of the automobile?
It was the model that, in 1908, marked the birth of the automobile industry. Its mechanical principles were much the same as those used today and it was clearly better than those of competing cars of that time. The Model T Ford was mass-produced at a low cost that made it very popular.

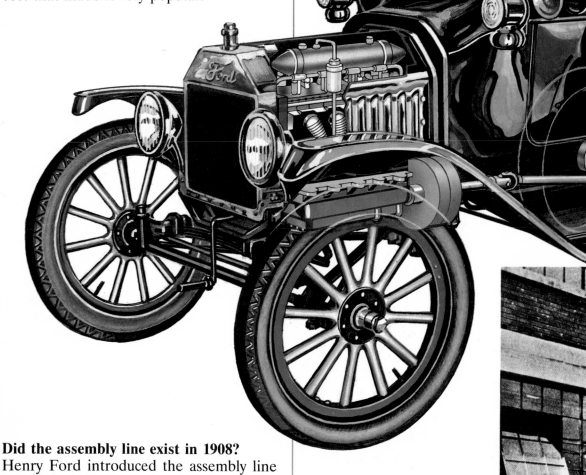

Did the assembly line exist in 1908?
Henry Ford introduced the assembly line into his Detroit factory for the construction of the Model T. The car advanced along the line from worker to worker as each one, in a mechanical fashion, performed the same function to each car. With this system Ford was able to produce his cars quickly and cheaply. The cars were so inexpensive that even the workers who built them could afford to buy them.

How many Model Ts were made?

The production of this car, which Americans called the *Tin Lizzie*, took place from 1908 to 1927. During this period the Ford Motor Company produced eighteen million of them. Prior to the production of the Model T, cars were expensive and were owned by a wealthy few. Because the Model T was so inexpensive, almost anyone could afford to buy it.

Was the Model T Ford the first mass-produced car?

No. The first mass-produced car was the Oldsmobile which was originally produced in 1901. But Olds, this car's maker, did not use the assembly line system, and his car did not reach a volume of production comparable to Henry Ford's.

Was the Model T the first Ford built?

No, Henry Ford had started to build automobiles many years before, in 1896.

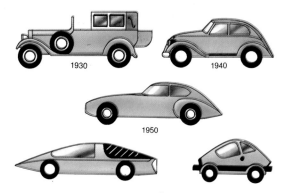

prototypes of modern cars

Has the shape of cars changed much since then?

Yes. The design of cars during that time was still much influenced by the old horse-drawn carriages. Above you can see designs from the 1930s, 1940s and 1950s, plus two modern-day prototype designs. The change in the shape of automobiles is toward lines that give better performance with lower fuel consumption.

MAGNETISM

What is magnetism?
The most common example of magnetism is the lodestone, the permanent natural magnet that attracts iron objects. This is only a large-scale example of a much more complex phenomenon found at the level of the atomic structure of matter which are linked to the phenomenon of electricity.

Does this mean that electricity and magnetism are always linked?
Yes, because everything in matter stems from the movement of electrons, which spin in orbit around the atomic nuclei. These electron movements are equivalent to small rings of electric current and create an electric field. Every electric field, however small, is associated with a magnetic field, which exerts its influence over a certain distance. The magnetic properties of materials depend on the various minute magnetic fields which are linked to the number of electrons present in an atom of the material. Each magnet has two poles: positive and negative. Opposite poles attract one another while poles which are alike repel.

Can the effect of a magnetic field be seen?
Yes. When placing a magnet amid some iron filings spread evenly on a sheet of paper you will actually see the filings arrange themselves in a particular pattern (see above photo). The lines along which the filings arrange themselves are the lines of force of the magnetic field.

What is an electro-magnet?
Lodestones are natural magnets but, because every electric field has an associated magnetic field, "artificial" magnets can be made. If an electric current is passed through a coil of wire, the coil acts like a temporary magnet and is able to magnetize a bar of iron within it; the more loops in the coil the stronger the magnetic field. This is the principle which huge electromagnets use to lift large masses of metal.

electromagnet

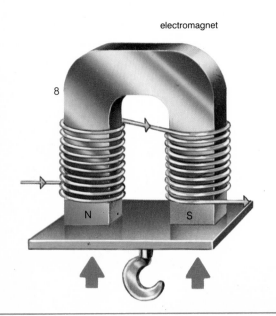

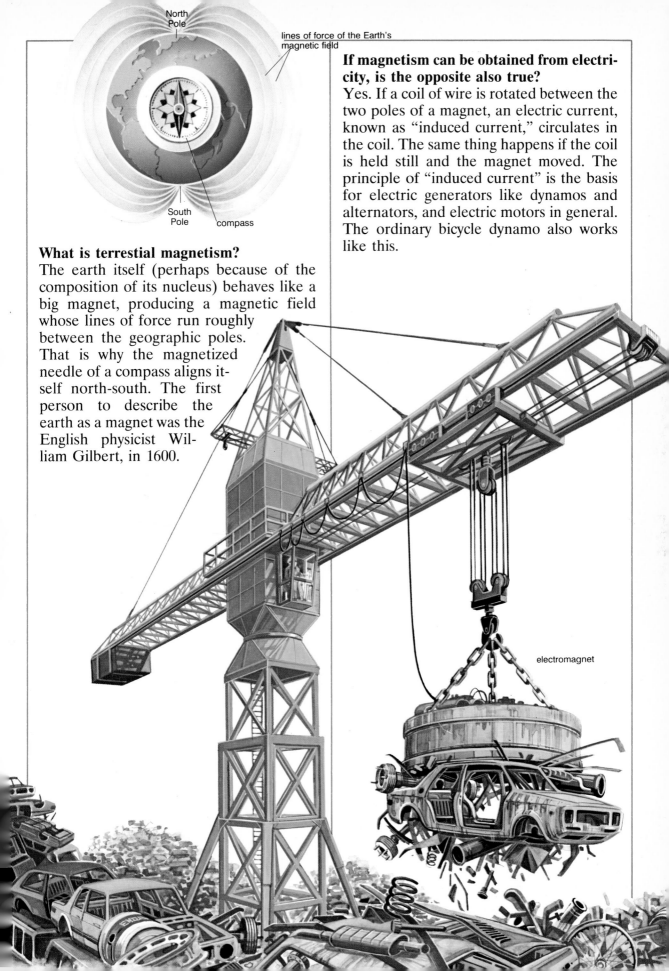

North Pole

lines of force of the Earth's magnetic field

South Pole

compass

What is terrestial magnetism?

The earth itself (perhaps because of the composition of its nucleus) behaves like a big magnet, producing a magnetic field whose lines of force run roughly between the geographic poles. That is why the magnetized needle of a compass aligns itself north-south. The first person to describe the earth as a magnet was the English physicist William Gilbert, in 1600.

If magnetism can be obtained from electricity, is the opposite also true?

Yes. If a coil of wire is rotated between the two poles of a magnet, an electric current, known as "induced current," circulates in the coil. The same thing happens if the coil is held still and the magnet moved. The principle of "induced current" is the basis for electric generators like dynamos and alternators, and electric motors in general. The ordinary bicycle dynamo also works like this.

electromagnet

MERCHANT SHIPS

What is a merchant ship?

In general any ship intended for commercial use on water (not just at sea, but also on inland waterways like rivers and lakes), is considered to be a merchant ship.

Are passenger ships considered merchant ships?

Yes. Merchant ships include those that: carry either passengers or cargo, perform work at sea or on the seabed (for example the laying of submarine cables), and service craft (such as tugs and hospital ships). In practice, all non-military vessels except pleasure craft are considered merchant ships.

What is a tanker?

A ship designed to carry liquid or gaseous cargo is called a tanker. The most important and biggest of these, the supertankers, are used for carrying oil or for the transport at low temperatures of liquid natural gas (methane). Some have a dead-weight capacity of up to 500,000 tons, and a length of over 1,000 feet.

What cargo did the Mississippi steamboats carry?

This type of ship was responsible for carrying mostly cotton and timber and also on occasion, passengers.

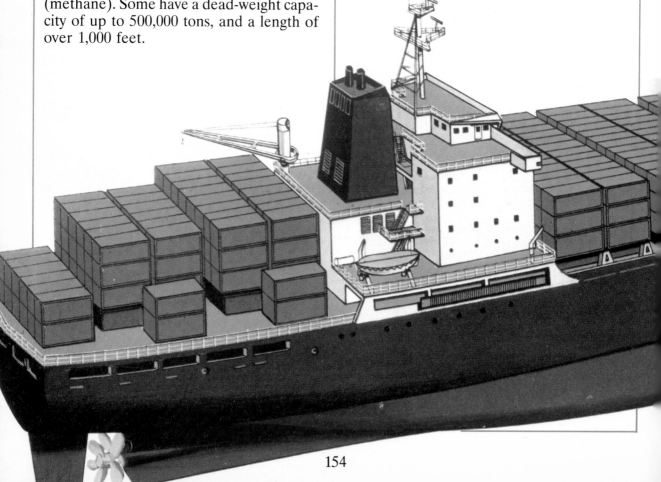

What is a container ship?

It is a particular kind of merchant ship, built to carry oblong containers of standard dimensions (with a volume of around 1,300 cubic feet). These are loaded on board by means of special cranes. The idea of the container was very simple, yet revolutionary, because the fixing of identical dimensions for all containers for all cargo has allowed the standardization of means of transport and methods of loading and unloading with great savings of time and scheduling. The same container can travel by road, rail or ship, reducing the problems of transfer between the different kinds of transport.

What is a tugboat?

It is special kind of merchant ship, designed to tow other vessels into places where they cannot maneuver themselves, or in cases of breakdown. They are also used for salvage

tugboat

operations as well as for work on lakes, lagoons and in ports.

In a modern container ship loading and unloading operations take place at the same time

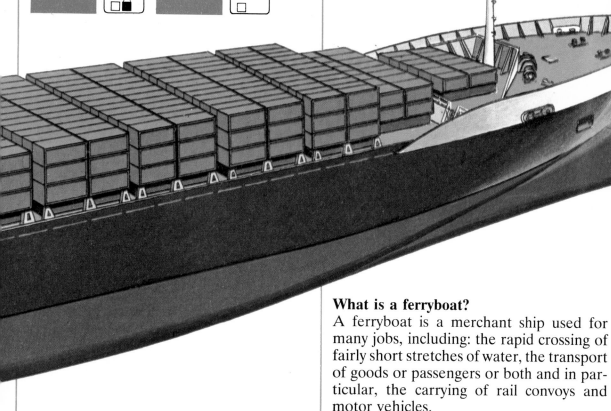

What is a ferryboat?

A ferryboat is a merchant ship used for many jobs, including: the rapid crossing of fairly short stretches of water, the transport of goods or passengers or both and in particular, the carrying of rail convoys and motor vehicles.

AIRSHIPS

What is an airship?

It is an aircraft that maintains itself in the air by aerostatic thrust because it is lighter than air. This is what makes airships different from airplanes, which are heavier than air and remain airborne by a different means, using "lift."

Does "lift" play any part in the flight of airships?

Unlike hot-air and gas balloons, the tapered shape of the airship also permits the aerodynamic use of "lift" (the thrust generated by air flowing more rapidly over than under the object moving through it).

Is a hot-air ballon an airship?

No, but hot-air balloons are also aerostatic; they remain airborne because they are lighter than air. Hot-air and other gas-filled balloons are lighter than aircraft but possess means of propulsion. They are moved only by air currents, while airships are equipped with motors, propellers and steering surfaces which control their flight.

Why is the airship *Norge* famous?

In 1926 the *Norge* was the first aircraft to fly over the North Pole. This famous expedition occurred at one-thirty Greenwich

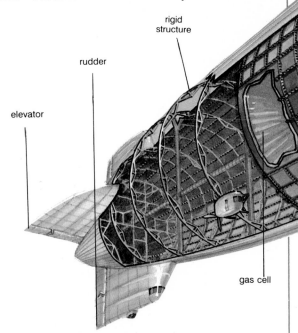

rigid structure

rudder

elevator

gas cell

Mean Time on the twelfth of May, in a flight that covered 3,300 miles from Spitsbergen to Teller in the Bering Sea (illustrated on the left). The *Norge* was designed and piloted by Umberto Nobile and the enterprise was the wish of the Norwegian explorer, Roald Amundsen, who in 1911 had already conquered the North Pole and in 1925 had unsuccessfully tried to fly over the North Pole in two seaplanes.

Which were the most successful airships?

The Zeppelins, built in Germany in 1914 and used by the German army in World War II for air raids and bombings, were the most successful of the airships.

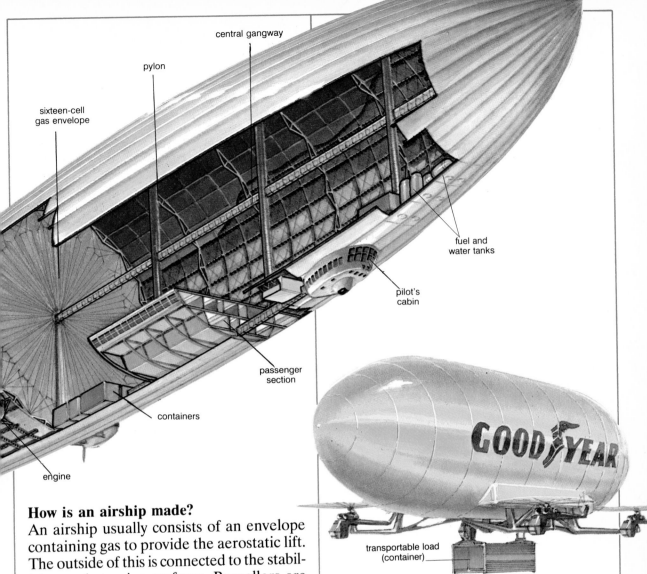

central gangway

pylon

sixteen-cell
gas envelope

fuel and
water tanks

pilot's
cabin

passenger
section

containers

engine

transportable load
(container)

How is an airship made?

An airship usually consists of an envelope containing gas to provide the aerostatic lift. The outside of this is connected to the stabilizing and steering surfaces. Propellers are suspended under the envelope as is the gondola which carries the cargo and passengers. The above section drawing shows the biggest rigid airship, the *Hindenburg*, of 1936. It was eight-hundred feet long and carried a load of twelve tons and fifty passengers.

Is the envelope always rigid?

There exist airships with rigid, semi-rigid as well as floppy envelopes.

What kind of gas is the envelope filled with?

Helium is usually used to fill airship envelopes. In the past, hydrogen was also used, but its inflammability caused many accidents, discouraging the continued use of it.

Are airships still used today?

Yes, airships are still used today but rarely for passengers or cargo even though they are among the aircraft with the greatest carrying capacity, especially for large, heavy loads. Since airships can remain in a fixed position, they are used to carry television cameras (for filming sporting events) and for monitoring areas in cases of fire or other disasters. They are also used for advertising and for communications. The drawing above shows a project for an airship for the transport of heavy loads. Propulsion will be provided by four helicopter engines.

TELECOMMUNICA-TIONS

Are there many types of long-distance communication?

There are basically three kinds of long-distance communication systems: acoustic, optical and electrical. The acoustic and optical systems are the most traditional. The voice, the drum and the signaling lamp, for example, were the first means of communication. However, modern telecommunication systems are based almost exclusively on electro-magnetism: when alternating current runs through a wire, magnetic waves are generated that travel through space like light waves.

How can we communicate using electro-magnetic waves?

Electro-magnetic waves travel long distances without weakening very much: the waves transmitted from an antenna can be received from long distances by a similar apparatus operating in reverse, transforming the magnetic waves back into measurable and interpretable electric current. Telegraph, telephone, radio and television all use this kind of wave.

telecommunications satellite

research laboratory

research laboratory

How is a message transmitted?

A simple, unchanging wave would certainly tell very little. The wave is altered, becoming what is called a "carrying wave" according to a pre-established code, by interrupting it or varying ("modulating") its length and frequency. The most simple case of this involves radio-telegraphy, in which a code with two signals, long and short, is enough. The systems for transmitting television images are more complex than this, but the same principle is applied.

Why are artificial satellites used for telecommunications?

Like light rays, radio waves are also reflected by obstacles: a satellite can act as a relay station and allow the exchange of messages between places that would otherwise be unable to communicate because of natural barriers.

What are the applications of satellites in telecommunications?

The most common applications include telephone, radio and television communications, but artificial satellites may carry sophisticated surveying instruments, and be able to relay data obtained by them back to earth. This is the typical application of meteorological satellites, which send constant information on conditions in the atmosphere and pictures taken by automatic television. Another interesting application of satellites is the communication between distant computers (one in Europe, the other in the United States, for example), which can put their computing resources into common programs to work together on the solution of problems that neither, working alone, could solve in the time available.

COMPUTERIZED ANIMATED CARTOONS

Is it difficult to make an animated cartoon?
The making of an animated cartoon is certainly a very long procedure. Besides the idea, the invention of scenes, characters and situations, the photographs for the film have to be prepared one by one. Images last for about a tenth of a second in our eyes, which means that to give the illusion of movement, ten images per second have to be projected. A little addition will tell you how many different drawings the artist must create, each one placed in exact sequence corresponding to the different phases of the movement, in order to make an animated cartoon that lasts even only a few minutes.

Can a computer be used to make animated cartoons?

Yes. To a certain point, today's artist can use a computer to create animated cartoons. The most typical case is the staging of images. Using a magnetic pencil, the artist confines himself to a few key drawings to portray a movement: the initial position, the intermediary and the final, as in the case presented on the left. He or she then prepares the scenario in which the action develops (below, on the right). By using these elements the computer's program enables it to generate all the images that give the illusion of movement, placed between those already given, with progressive changes in the initial image to bring it toward the intermediary one, and so on. This method of working is faster.

Is this the only technique for which the computer is used?

No. Many special effects, not only in animated cartoons, but also in films and advertising, are achieved by means of the computer. When, for example, you see writing that rotates, lengthens, broadens or becomes distorted, the effect generally is obtained through a graphic computer program. The same is true of the special effects in adventure and science-fiction-films.

An image can be taken and turned into a form "understandable" to the computer, for instance, conversion into a series of numbers, to which the computer can make all kinds of changes. This results in a reconverted image useable in a film.

Are the computer's drawings always perfect?

Not all of the computer's drawings will be perfect. It depends on the complexity of the insertions asked of the computer, and on the sophistication of the program written for it. For the moment, some retouching by the artist is usually necessary.

Is *Mickey Mouse* still popular today?

Mickey Mouse, created by the imagination of Walt Disney for his comic strips in 1930, is still, together with *Donald Duck*, the animated cartoon character most loved by children.

ELECTRONIC GAMES

What are electronic games?

Electronics have in recent years spread further and further into our lives. It would be difficult to imagine a world without television sets, radios or computers. Electronics also make space exploration possible. It was therefore inevitable that electronics should affect the world of toys. We can find an ever-growing number of electronic games: naval battles, Star Wars, football, quizzes, etc. Many of these can be played on the computer. For example, computers exist that can play chess because the programmer has taught it all the rules of the game, all the consequences of each move and the counter-moves. In the same way computers can play football or naval battles (below).

What are video games?

Video games are played on the computer and appear on the colored television screen. There exist games of various kinds, including those for intelligence, different skills, educational and even trivia video games. The program of the game is contained on a cassette or disc which is loaded into the computer.

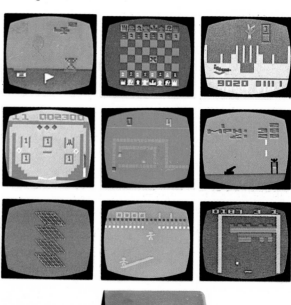

How many kinds of computers are used for games?

There are two kinds of computers generally used for games: central computers (used simultaneously by many people) and personal computers designed for one or two players. The games that can be played on the first are very complex and can include words and even logic. They often take the form of adventure stories in which the player must solve a mystery or find a hidden treasure. Personal computers are used more for sports and other more visual games. The games can be loaded on to discs and added to the computer's memory.

How do you play a game on the personal computer?

The most common way of playing a game on a personal computer is by moving a special command lever called the "joystick" which is plugged into the machine. Some computer games are played by only one

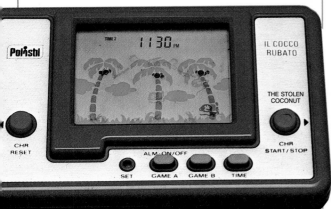

contestant against the computer, while others can be played by two or more at the same time. In some sports games, for example, the computer will take the place of a player if one is absent. In general, the best games for personal computers are those that combine logic with lively pictures and visual action.

Who invented Lego?

Alongside the highly sophisticated electronic toys that we have just discussed, there are more traditional ones, like construction games, which stimulate children's imagination and inventiveness. The most popular building game is Lego. This was invented by Kirk Christiansen, who had the idea of making the first interlocking bricks. With these bricks and other elements, together with some imagination, it is possible to make the most varied constructions from a simple house to an enchanted castle from the latest car to a spaceship.

Is Legoland like Disneyland?

Lego is so famous that in Denmark there is a park with a city called *Legoland*, in which you can find houses half as high as a man, fantastic towns and a zoo with animals from all over the world.

The Rocket

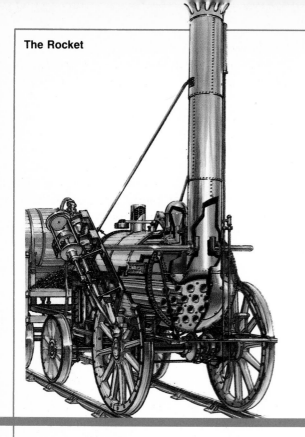

TGV (Train Grande Vitesse – "High Speed Train")

TRAINS

How did the first locomotives work?

The first locomotives, which appeared at the beginning of the nineteenth century, were steam-powered, and obtained energy through using coal. They were very slow, and technical progress replaced them with electric and diesel locomotives.

When did the electric locomotive appear?

Electric locomotives appeared at the end of the nineteenth century. The major problem with the use of these locomotives was the need to install and efficiently maintain a whole electrical system for the railway, including generators, sub-stations and a network of electric cables along the lines. The locomotive gets the electrical energy it needs through a pantograph, a retractible device for collecting current that is mounted on the roof of the locomotive. The illustration shows an Austrian electric locomotive.

pantograph

radio antenna

warning horn

buffers

Which was the fastest of the first steam locomotives?

The *Rocket*, which you see illustrated on the left of the opposite page, was the fastest of the first steam locomotives. This locomotive, built by Robert Stephenson in 1829, and used on the Liverpool-Manchester line, could reach the speed (incredible for the time) of 29 miles per hour. The complete steam locomotive is composed of the driving vehicle, where the boiler is installed, with an accompanying car (the tender), which carries the fuel and water for the boiler. The *Rocket* and the Liverpool-Manchester line served as a model for the development of the railway the world over.

What is the TGV?

The TGV (illustration on the right of the opposite page), the Train Grande Vitesse, or "High Speed Train," is a train developed by the French Railways. Its service runs on the Paris-Lyons line, which it covers in two hours, forty minutes at a speed of 162 miles per hour. The TGV is made up of eight cars placed between two locomotives. The wheels are no longer found under, but instead are between the cars, and run on new, specially built tracks. The speed record of this train, which is the fastest in the world, at 1236 miles per hour, was established in February 1981.

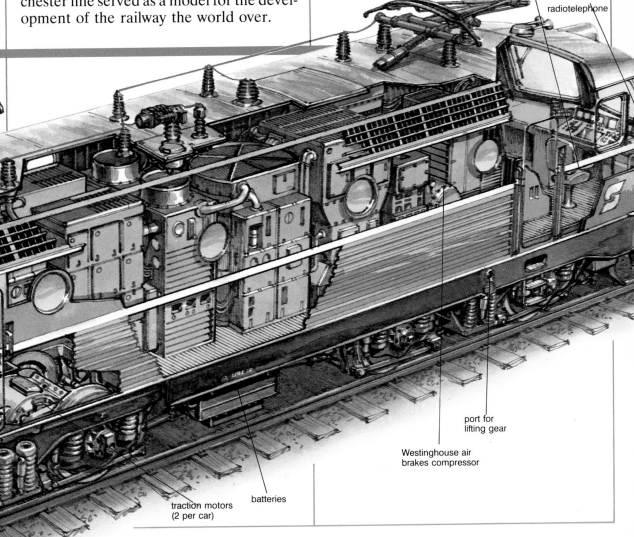

driver's station

radiotelephone

port for lifting gear

Westinghouse air brakes compressor

batteries

traction motors (2 per car)

ENERGY SOURCES

What is energy?

When any object moves it uses energy. Any work therefore requires the use of energy. In the case of humans, energy is provided by muscular strength. In practice, energy carries out any activity.

What were the first sources of energy?

Man learned from very early times how to extract energy from natural sources such as wind and water. He also depended on the muscular strength of animals as well as his own, to provide needed energy. Mills equipped with blades were moved by the flow of water or by the wind; these put into motion mechanisms that provided energy that replaced the energy of humans or animals. With the progress of technology, these systems have been improved. Hydroelectric stations, for example, still use the force of falling water to provide needed energy.

When were other sources discovered?

With the Industrial Revolution of the seventeenth century, coal began to be used and later in the twentieth century, oil began to provide energy. By burning these natural resources, energy is released which drives machines to produce goods more quickly.

						SOLAR		
WIND			WAVES		RIVER FLOWS	THERMAL HEAT	DIRECT HEAT	PH EF
windmill	wind-driven generator	sailboat	floating generator worked by wave motion	watermill	hydroelectric power station	ocean thermal electricity conversion station	solar collector power station	p p

What is geothermal energy?

The enormous heat generated by the white-hot magma beneath the earth's crust often escapes in the form of huge jets of steam, called "geysers". Geysers are potential sources of energy. In Iceland, for example, they are widely used for heating houses.

Is there also such a thing as chemical energy?

The chemical reactions which occur between substances are generators of energy. Often these reactions generate energy in the form of electricity. This is the case with batteries, where electricity is produced as a result of the reaction between zinc and ammonium chloride. Other substances used to generate electrical energy are silver, nickel and cadmium.

Are there other sources of energy?

In the middle of the twentieth century a powerful source of energy was discovered within the atom. Nuclear power stations are now trying to use this form of energy to its fullest advantage. Unfortunately, the use of nuclear power creates many problems. These range from the use of the energy itself, (it is the basis for the destructive fare of the atomic bomb) to disposing of the radio-active waste material produced by the splitting of the atom. In recent years, we have also been using new technologies to make more rational use of old forms of natural energy, such as the wind, water and, especially, the sun. Indeed, the enormous forces present in our solar system seem capable of providing us with new sources of energy.

FOOD	WOOD	OIL, CARBON FUELS, NATURAL GAS	BIOMASS	SUB-TERRANEAN ROCKS AND HOT SPRINGS	GRAVITA-TIONAL TIDES
conversion into muscular energy	burning of firewood	steam generators, heating of buildings	chemical conversion of vegetable matter, organic waste etc. into fuels	geothermal power station	tidal power station

THE ENERGY
OF THE ATOM

What is the structure of an atom?
The atom is a bit like a miniature solar system containing a nucleus at the center and particles, called electrons, which move around it.

How is atomic energy obtained?
There are two different ways of obtaining energy directly from an atom: an atom can be split into two lighter atoms, or two atoms can be joined into one heavier one. The two processes are called, respectively, *fission* and *fusion*. Both fission and fusions cause the release of large amounts of energy because during these reactions a part of the original mass disappears and converts itself completely into energy.

Are atomic energy and nuclear energy the same thing?
Yes, they are but it is more correct to refer to these processes as nuclear energy, because in the reactions of fission and fusion only the nuclei, not the entire atom are involved. The "missing" mass that is converted into energy comes from the nuclei.

What is a chain reaction?
When an atom undergoes fission it splits into two simpler atoms, releasing large quantities of energy and often also neutrons, which are emitted at high velocity and can collide with other atomic nuclei, causing the fission of these. The new nuclei also emit neutrons which collide with other atoms, and so on. Once triggered off, the first reaction produces other, "chain" reactions. This is why a nuclear reaction can become explosive, as in the case of the Atomic Bomb.

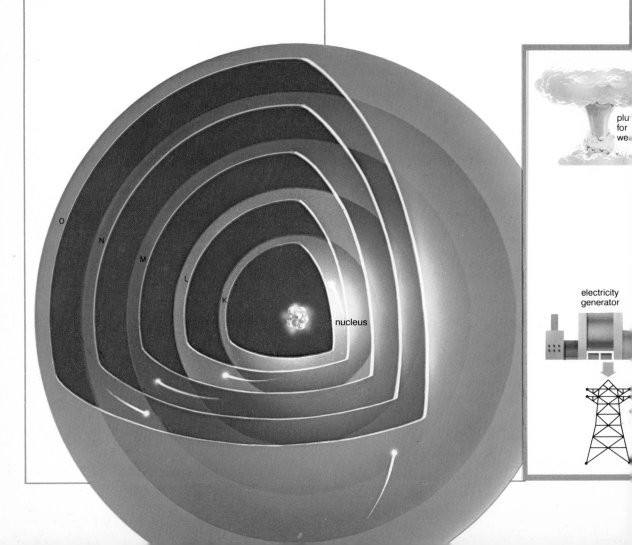

nucleus

plu
for
we

electricity
generator

What elements are used to produce nuclear reactions?

Nuclear fission reactions were discovered by experimentally bombarding the nuclei of uranium, one of the elements in which it is easiest to produce fission causing a great release of energy. In general, the elements most easily split are the heaviest elements of thorium: those most used are the various isotopes of uranium and plutonium. On the other hand lighter elements are used in fusion. Commonly used are hydrogen and its isotopes, which fuse to produce helium nuclei.

Is it true that the sun's energy is caused by nuclear fusion reactions?

Yes. Not only the sun, but stars in general get their energy from the fusion of hydrogen nuclei. Part of the energy released from the sun reaches the earth in the forms of light and heat.

USES OF NUCLEAR ENERGY

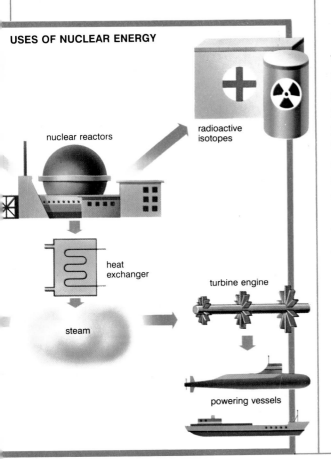

nuclear reactors

radioactive isotopes

heat exchanger

turbine engine

steam

powering vessels

What are the uses of nuclear energy now?

Unfortunately, military uses are still dominant as the superpowers have built up enormous stockpiles of nuclear weapons. The main peacetime use of nuclear energy is for the generation of electricity in nuclear power stations. Here the nuclear reactions are controlled in the reactors and used to produce thermal heat: water is heated and the steam generated drives turbines that convert the thermal energy into electric energy. Another peaceful application of atomic energy is the use of radioactive isotopes in medicine.

Is it true that there are nuclear submarines?

Yes, there are nuclear submarines and ships which house small nuclear reactors that produce all the energy each vessel needs. The first nuclear submarine was the *Nautilus*, built in the United States of America and launched in 1955.

OIL

What is oil made of?
If millions of years ago the planet had not been inhabited by animals and covered by plants, we would not have oil, a basic source of energy for human activity today. It was the decomposition of these organisms, later buried deep in the earth and subjected to a series of chemical changes, that created the black, sticky liquid we know as oil. Oil is therefore a combination of several elements known as hydrocarbons.

What contributed to chemical change?
The organic substances were pushed down deeper by terrestrial movements and the settling of the earth's crust. The weight of rock and the high temperature at the center of the earth brought about the mixing and fusion of these substances.

Where are oil deposits found?
They are found at various depths, depending on geological structure. Because of its specific weight, oil tends to rise to the surface. It is blocked only when it meets solid rock. There are cases in which it surfaces naturally, as in the vast lakes formed in the Middle East. But in most cases the extraction of oil requires the formation of artificial wells by drilling.

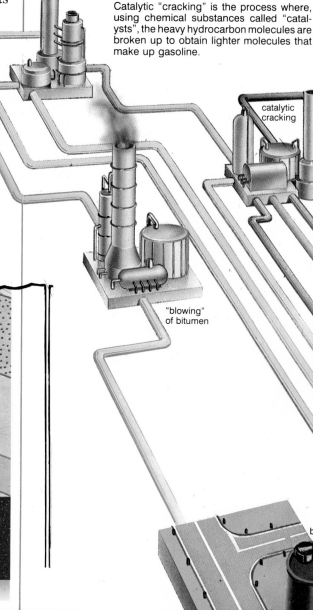

Catalytic "cracking" is the process where, using chemical substances called "catalysts", the heavy hydrocarbon molecules are broken up to obtain lighter molecules that make up gasoline.

catalytic cracking

"blowing" of bitumen

bitum

alluvium

clay overburden

80% gas
20% water

80% oil
20% water

20% oil   salt water   20% water

Can oil be used immediately?

The viscous liquid extracted from the earth is no longer used as "crude," in the form in which it comes out of the earth. It is subjected to a process of preparation, the purpose of which is to separate the different components. This process is carried out in refineries, which may be located near the oilfields, but are more often a considerable distance away, or even overseas. In the first case oil pipelines are built to carry the oil; in the second, enormous oil tankers are used to transport it.

How is crude oil processed?

It is processed by distillation and refining. The crude oil is pumped into tanks that are vertically divided into compartments. By applying heat which gradually reduces in temperature from the bottom upward, lighter and lighter derivatives are obtained. These range from bitumen, used for asphalt, to gas and benzine. Each new element obtained is then, with new processes, further refined and made ready for use (illustration below).

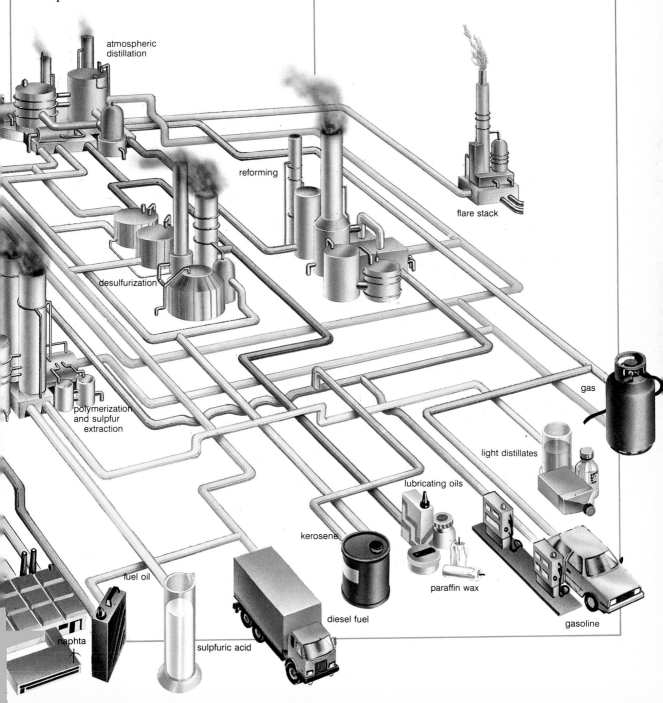

atmospheric distillation

reforming

flare stack

desulfurization

polymerization and sulfur extraction

gas

light distillates

lubricating oils

kerosene

paraffin wax

fuel oil

diesel fuel

gasoline

naphta

sulphuric acid

HEAT AND TEMPERATURE

What is heat?
Heat is a form of energy: the energy of movement (kinetic energy) of atoms and particles makes heat. Applying heat to an object increases the movement of the atoms which comprise it by giving energy to them.

What is radiation?
Radiation is another form of heat distribution. If we turn on the radiator or light a fire in a fireplace the air in the room will be warmed by convection. If we place our hands on a radiator they, too are warmed by conduction. If on the other hand we hold our hands at a distance from the fire they are warmed by radiation.

conduction · convection · radiation

What is heat conduction?
It is the usual way heat is transmitted through solid objects without changing their composition. If, for example, the end of a metal bar is placed close to a flame, the other end will also be heated: the heat passes through the bar by conduction.

What is convection?
This is the way heat is transmitted through fluids which occurs through the movement of matter. The water at the bottom of a receptacle placed on a flame heats first: it becomes less dense and lighter, and therefore rises. Equilibrium is reached as the movement continues. Heat distribution by convection occurs in liquids and gases.

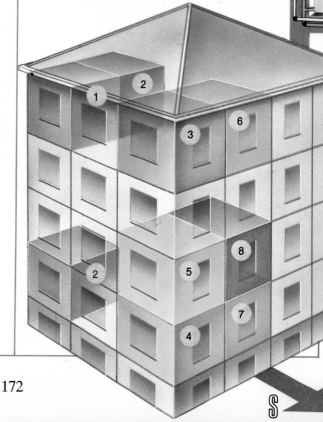

expansion tank

hot
water

cold
water

boiler

How does central heating work?
A boiler (usually located in the basement) heats water which rises (or is pumped) through the pipes leading to upper rooms or apartments, where they impart heat by conduction to the radiators, which then give off heat through radiation and convection. The premises exposed to the south (from 3 to 8 in the illustration) need less heat than those exposed to the north (1 and 2) because they usually receive more sunlight (natural heat).

Are temperature and heat the same things?
No! Heat is a form of energy, while temperature is a physical measure that indicates the thermal condition of something, and which comes from the physical sensation (subjective) of hot and cold that we experience through touching things. There is a strict relationship between heat and temperature (heat must be applied to a body to raise its temperature), but the two should not be confused.

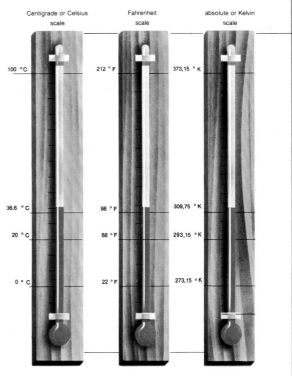

Centigrade or Celsius scale	Fahrenheit scale	absolute or Kelvin scale
100 °C	212 °F	373,15 °K
36.6 °C	98 °F	309,75 °K
20 °C	68 °F	293,15 °K
0 °C	22 °F	273,15 °K

What is temperature measured with?
The temperature of a substance is measured by thermometric scales, based on so-called fundamental intervals, fixed points at which principal physical phenomena occur. The Celsius or Centigrade scale fixes at zero degrees, the freezing point of water and at one hundred degrees, its boiling point and divides this interval into one hundred equal degrees. The Fahrenheit scale, similar to Celsius, is used mainly in the United States and Canada. The Kelvin scale measures absolute temperatures and is used in the scientific field.

FORMULA 1 RACING CARS

Is it true that Formula 1 racing cars today have engines which generate eight hundred to nine hundred horse power?

Today's cars may have engines which generate eight hundred – nine hundred horsepower in racing; in testing 1,200 horsepower can be reached. The maximum cylinder capacity for these cars is a hundred and eighty centimeters for aspirated engines, which drops to ninety centimeters for turbocharged engines (where the air for the fuel mixture is compressed before entering the cylinders). Speeds reached are now around two-hundred-and-twenty miles per hour; during racing, average speeds exceed one-hundred-and-twenty miles per hour. The structure of Formula 1 cars is strictly controlled by rules which fix the weight and dimensions of each car. The Formula 1 car seen in the section below is the Ferrari 312 T4, driven by Jody Scheckter, which won the world championship in 1979.

1911 Marmon Wasp

When did car racing start?

The first race goes back to 1894, when the Paris daily newspaper, *Le Petit Journal*, awarded a prize for the "horseless carriage" that had covered the distance from Paris to Rouen (78 miles), "with reasonable cost and with ease of handling." A score of cars had contested the prize on July 22, 1894. The first to arrive was the Comte de Dion's steam carriage, which completed the course at an average speed of eleven-and-two tenths of a mile per hour, but did not win the prize because it was hard to steer and weighed over two tons, and needed 1,760 pounds of fuel to run.

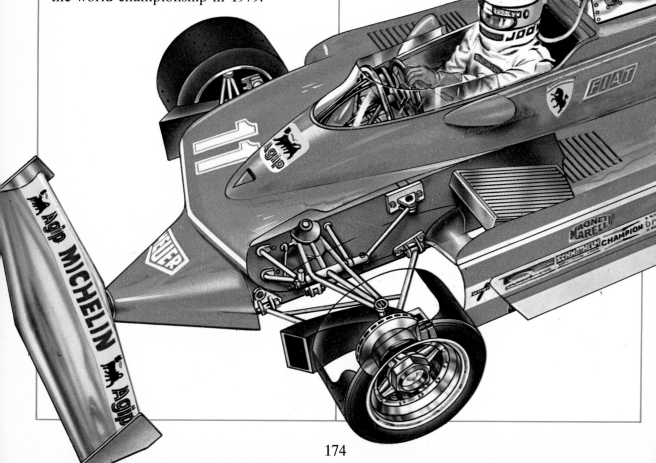

1950 Alfa Romeo (Alfetta)

1951 Ferrari

1957 Maserati

1970 Lotus-Ford

1980 Williams

Who won the first world championship?

The first Formula 1 world championship was held in 1950. It was won by Nino Farina in an Alfa Romeo.

Why are these cars called "Formula 1"?

Until 1906 races were open to any kind of automobile. Only from that year on were the "Formulas" defined by the characteristics (weight, cylinder capacity, fuel consumption, etc.) of cars allowed to participate in each particular race. Now there are various formulas and many kinds of races.

Is the type of tire important for Formula 1 cars?

At the speeds attained in racing, part played by the tires in assuring perfect grip on the track is vital. The tire seen on the Ferrari is a "slick" for a dry track; above is a "rain," wet weather tire.

THE KING OF METALS

What are "noble" metals?

These are chemically inactive metals that resist chemical change and include gold, silver, platinum, palladium, ruthenium, rhodium, iridium, osmium and mercury. Gold is the softest and most pliable of these metals: it can be beaten into sheets as thick as four thousandths of an inch.

When was gold first used?

The Sumerians in the fourth millennium B.C. used gold to make jewelry, and then the Egyptians used it, especially for their funerary ornaments (below, the pure gold mask of Tutankhamen and, right, the golden temple of Pagan in Burma). The use of gold as money goes back to the second millennium B.C.: pieces of gold were exchanged by weight. The first gold coins appeared in some Ionic cities in the seventh century, B.C.

Where is gold found?

The roundish lumps, nuggets and gold dust, auriferous sand, are found in two kinds of deposit. In "primary deposits" gold-bearing rock is mixed with other rocks rich in quartz. In "alluvial" deposits gold is mixed with sand from the erosion of the primary deposits. Most of the auriferous deposits are in South Africa, the Urals, Siberia, California and Columbia.

How is the extracted mineral treated?

The extracted gold is powdered and washed, then put through the "cyanide process," which separates it from the "gangue," and all the other minerals it is mixed with. It is then melted down. Below are ingots of unrefined gold.

What are the characteristics of gold?

Pure gold possesses considerable electrical conductivity, does not oxidize under heat, and melts at 9,727 degrees Celsius. It resists most chemical attacks, except that of chlorine, bromine and aqua regia. It has a high resistance to corrosion and is used in chemical apparatus, in laboratories, and in some electrical circuits. It is also used as a shield against harmful radiation.

How is gold used?

Because pure gold is soft it is used mostly in alloys with other metals, such as copper, silver, platinum and nickel. The addition of up to 10% of copper, for example, hardens gold without reducing its flexibility. The alloys are used chiefly for coinage and jewelry. "White gold" is an alloy of 80% of gold with 20% of platinum and is used in dentistry as well as for jewelry.

What is a carat?

It is the unit of measure of gold content: the number of carats gives the number of parts of pure gold in twenty-four parts of alloy. For example, eighteen-carat gold contains eighteen parts of pure gold and six parts of another metal.

How are the other "noble" metals used?

Pure silver is used for salts, silver nitrate in pharmacy, and in the bromide for photographic film. In nature, platinum is often found among metals of the same group (ruthenium, rhodium, palladium, osmium and iridium). It is used in combination with these, which are often used as catalysts, substances that alter the speed of a chemical reaction. Mercury is a "nearly" noble metal which, at temperatures over three hundred degrees Celsius (one-hundred-and-thirteen degrees Fahrenheit), combines with oxygen. We all know its uses in thermometers and barometers.

COLOR

What is color?
Color is a quality that people see with their eyes which happens when an object is struck by a light beam or spectrum.

What is the spectrum?
If you break up white light by passing it through a prism and project the radiating rays on a screen, a continuous strip of different colors appears. The spectrum of sunlight is a luminous band made up of seven basic colors: indigo, violet, blue, green, yellow, red and orange.

What does the color of things depend on?
Objects have the property of absorbing some colors and reflecting others. It is only those which reflect that we see. An object looks red because it has absorbed all the other colors contained in white light and reflected only red; if it looks black it means that it has absorbed all the colors, and if white, that it has absorbed none and reflected them all.

What makes different colors?
Colors are determined by the different wavelengths, λ, emitted by light. These are measured in angstroms, Å, and those visible to the human eye run from 4000 Å (violet), to 7000 Å (red), as shown in the diagram at the bottom of the page. Light waves, unlike water or sound, travel through space in concentric motion, as shown in the diagram, and their fundamental characteristics are "frequency", the number of cycles in a given period of time, and "fullness" the height of the top of the arc.

Do all living creatures see color?
Only human beings and a few animals see colors. Among the animals that see colors are the primates, butterflies, bees, fish, amphibians, some reptiles and some birds. Color is perceived by man through the cone-shaped organs in the retina of the eyes. There are some people who are missing some or all of the cones. They cannot see in color and are considered to be "colorblind."

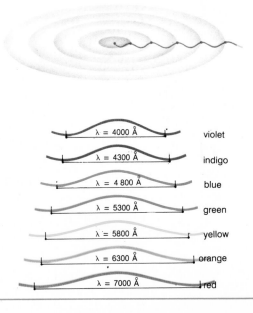

$\lambda = 4000$ Å	violet
$\lambda = 4300$ Å	indigo
$\lambda = 4800$ Å	blue
$\lambda = 5300$ Å	green
$\lambda = 5800$ Å	yellow
$\lambda = 6300$ Å	orange
$\lambda = 7000$ Å	red

What are the characteristics of color?

There are three basic characteristics of color: hue, which depends solely on the wave length; saturation, which depends on the lesser or greater amount of white light mixed with the color; brightness, which depends on the greater or lesser capacity of a colored surface to reflect light. The primary colors are blue, yellow and red; by mixing them you can get all the other colors, but you cannot get a primary color by mixing the others.

How are colors made?

In a dark room three projectors with different colors, green, red and violet-blue, are switched on at the same time. By overlapping the red and violet rays you will get "magenta," red and green make yellow, violet and green make azure-blue. Where all three beams overlap you will have white.

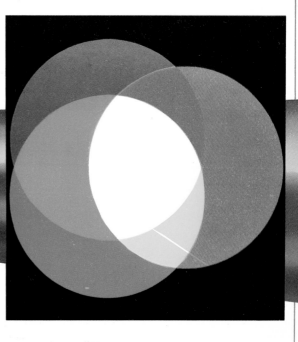

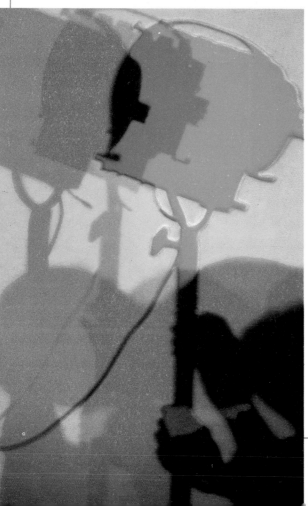

What is a shadow?

Shadow is a dark area produced by a solid mass which intercepts the rays emitted by the light source and blocks their passage. Shade is, therefore, strictly linked to light, and will vary in color according to the color of the light producing it. If an object is lit by a beam of white light, the shadow cast by it will be black; if, however, we use a beam of red light, the color of the shadow will be blue. In the same way green light will give a magenta shadow, and violet light a yellow one. If three colored lights are switched on at the same time there will be shadows of different colors.

179

DID YOU KNOW...?

Where does *tar* come from?
Tar, a thick black substance used to repair roads, comes from the distillation of coal, wood and other organic materials.

What is *TNT*?
TNT is the abbreviation for trinitrotoluene. It is a chemical compound used to make explosives and rocket fuel.

What does *caliber* mean?
Caliber is the diameter of the inside of the barrel of a firearm (a pistol, a rifle, or a cannon). It can also be the diameter of the outside of a bullet.

What does an *altimeter* do?
This device is used to measure the height of one point in relationship to another. In a glider plane, for example, an altimeter measures the height of the plane in relationship to the ground.

What does the *diaphragm* in a camera do?
The diaphragm, located behind the lens, is a mechanism that opens and closes, controlling the amount of light entering the lens. If the light is very strong, the diaphragm will not open as wide.

What is *firedamp*?
It is a gaseous mixture of air and methane that, if lit by a match, will cause a huge explosion. It is easily produced in coal and sulphur mining.

Why has *DDT* been banned?
The molecules of this powerful insecticide are virtually indestructible. Because of this, they are a threat to the ecological balance of nature. Its use was prohibited in 1969.

What is a *derrick*?
It is a pyramid-shaped metal structure that supports the drills and pipes of an oil well.

What is a *breakwater*?
Breakwaters are stone barriers that protect a port, harbor or beach from the force of the sea.

What is *dioxin*?
It is a highly toxic chemical that is not biodegradable. It has been used in herbicides and is now believed to cause cancer.

How fast can a *hover-train* go?
The "hover-train" is a train that travels over a cushion of air, using special reinforced concrete tracks shaped like an upside-down T. It can reach speeds of up to 250 miles per hour.

What is a *charter flight*?
It is a passenger plane that has been hired for use on a particular day by a group of people or a company. A ticket usually costs less than it would for a regular commercial flight.

What is a *fax machine*?
"Fax" is a nickname for facsimile transceiver. It is an electronic mailing system that allows you to send letters over the telephone in a matter of minutes. The letter is fed into a machine in one place, is "read" using electrical impulses, and is reproduced through a receiving machine somewhere else.

What is a *holograph*?
It is a photographic technique that allows a three-dimensional image to be projected. It can be seen from many different points of view as if it were a real object.

What is a *container*?
It is a standard-sized metal receptacle used for the shipment of goods by land, sea or air.

What do *starboard* and *port* mean?
These terms refer to the two sides of a ship. When facing the front of the boat, "port" is the side to the left and "starboard" is the side to the right.

What is a *burin* used for?
A burin is a steel engraving tool. It has a pointed shaft and is used to carve and engrave gold, silver, copper and even leather.

Are there any *airplanes* that can fly without the use of engines?
Yes, there are lighter-than-air dirigibles like the blimp, the semi-rigid airship and the zeppelin that fly but do not have engines. They use gas carried in a huge bag to lift the ship and possess some form of propulsion. There are also heavier-than-air aircraft that depend on aerodynamic forces for power. This group includes glider and sail planes.

What is a *cement mixer*?
It is a machine with a big revolving tilted drum that is used for the preparation of concrete.

What do *AM* and *FM* mean?
These terms refer to two kinds of signals that a radio sends out to its listeners. AM signals are used for standard broadcasts while FM signals are on a higher frequency band. *FM* are signals free from noise and other interference that can affect AM signals.

What is a *sounding machine*?
It is an instrument used to measure the depth of a body of water. At one time, a sounding machine simply consisted of a rope with knots placed along its length and a weight attached to the end. Today sounding machines can measure temperature and take water samples as well.

What is a *compact disc*?
A compact disc plays music like an ordinary record. However, CDs, as they are also called, are discs that are only four-and-one-half inches in diameter, as opposed to the twelve inches of ordinary records. Instead of grooves, CDs have millions of tiny indentations and flat zones. They are read by a laser beam instead of a needle. The laser searches the surface of the disc, reads the pattern of indentations and flat zones and transforms them into electric signals and then into vibrations which produce sound.

What does *LASER* mean?
LASER stands for "Light Amplification by Stimulated Emission of Radiation."

What is a *laser*?
The laser, invented in 1960, produces a very special kind of light. The light waves that it produces all proceed in the same direction and many have the same wavelength. The laser is very powerful. It can cut steel plates as if they were butter. It is often used in surgery.

Who invented the *first calculator*?
It was invented by Charles Babbage in 1821. It had so many gears and it was so complicated that it was not possible to get all of it to work at once.

At what speed does *light* travel?
Light travels at an enormous speed. It moves at precisely 186,282,396 miles per second. This is more than 42,000 times faster than the Concord can fly.

Why are there no fires on the *moon*?
There are no fires on the moon because there is no oxygen. Without oxygen nothing can burn.

What is the force of gravity on the *moon*?
The moon is much smaller than the earth and the force of gravity is only one-sixth what it is here. On the moon, you can jump six times as high and throw a ball six times farther than on earth.

HOW, WHERE, WHEN AND WHY

Where does *chewing gum* come from?

In the Yucatan forests and in Guatemala, there is a tree, the sapodilla, that contains a special sap. This sap is extracted by making deep cuts into the tree's bark. The thick milk or sap is then boiled and becomes elastic. By adding flavors to it, like mint, banana and cinnamon, we eventually get commercial brands of chewing gum.

Who invented the first *folding umbrella*?

The first folding umbrella was invented by an Englishman, Mr. Holland from Birmingham, in 1851.

What are *X-rays*?

They are rays that are able to pass through a solid, opaque body and produce an image on a photographic plate. Thanks to x-rays, we can now take pictures of the human skeleton from the outside. They were discovered by a German physicist, Wilhelm Rontgen, in 1895.

What is a *saxophone*?

It is a musical wind instrument invented by a Belgian, Adolphe Sax. Saxophones are especially used to play jazz music. There are two types of saxophones, the tenor sax and the soprano sax.

What was the *Boston Tea Party*?

In December, 1773, tea had the leading role in an important historical event. In Boston, American colonists protested against the taxes placed on them by the British government. Rebelling against British demands, some of the colonists refused to load the ships and threw a load of tea into the harbor. This was one of the acts that led to the Revolutionary War. Today this act is known as the Boston Tea Party.

Who was the first woman to climb *Mont Blanc*?

In 1808, Marie Paradis was the first woman to conquer Mont Blanc.

What are *hiccups*?

Sometimes, our diaphragm contracts involuntarily. At the same time our larynx and throat also close, stopping the air from going out for a moment. This causes us to hiccup.

Who invented the *phonograph*?

Thomas Alva Edison patented the phonograph in 1877. A metal needle attached to a membrane engraved sound vibrations onto a cylinder covered with tin. Grooves were made as the sound was recorded. Then, when a needle moved over these grooves, the vibrations were reproduced. They were then magnified to form sounds which could be heard.

What are *colorings*?
They are substances that give a stable color to a material or an object. In the past, they were extracted from plants and animals but today they are usually made from chemicals. They are used, for instance, to color, Easter eggs or the icing on a birthday cake.

Who was *Adonis*?
Adonis was a beautiful young Greek loved by the goddess, Aphrodite. When he died, she convinced the god, Zeus, to let Adonis leave the underworld for six months every year and stay with her. The time he spent in the underworld became the season of winter while the time he spent with Aphrodite became summer.

What is a *fresco*?
A fresco is a painting that is made when a moist plaster wall surface is decorated with colors dissolved in water or limewater.

What is *UNICEF*?
It stands for United Nations Children's Fund. It was created in 1946 to improve the living conditions of children, particularly those in developing, war-ridden countries or countries devastated by natural disasters.

Is a *prairie chicken* a bird?
Yes, it is a kind of game bird that lives in the Great Plains. A prairie chicken has brownish feathers with black or brown stripes.

Is it true that the *electric eel* produces electricity?
Yes. By using its tail, the electric eel can stun its prey with a charge from 450 to 600 volts.

Are *lizards* reptiles?
Yes. Lizards usually have four legs and are covered with scales. Geckos, iguanas, chameleons and gila monsters are all lizards. Lizards, like all reptiles, are also cold-blooded.

What is the *biggest lizard* in the world?
The biggest lizard known to man is the Komodo dragon, one of the monitor lizards living in Southeast Asia. It can grow up to ten feet long and weigh three hundred pounds.

Where does *cork* come from?
It is the thick bark of a cork oak tree that grows in the Mediterranean.

What is the *biggest land mollusk*?
It is the giant snail found in Malaysia, Thailand, Indonesia, Vietnam, the Philippines and China. It can grow to be eight inches long. Like many mollusks, the giant snail has a soft body and a hard shell.

Is it true that there is a *plant* that looks like a rock?
Yes, it is called the rock plant. The body of the plant looks like a rock. It has two fleshy leaves that fit together, and grows in rocky places in southern Africa. It is very hard to spot. When it flowers, the two leaves open and let out a long bud. This opens into a beautiful yellow or white flower.

How did *blue jeans* get their name?
In 1851, a German named Levi Strauss arrived in California with rolls of a rugged blue material. He was going to make tents

for the gold miners. But the miners wanted sturdy trousers, not tents. Instead Strauss made trousers with his material and they have been worn ever since. This kind of material had been used since the fifteenth century by sailors from Genoa. The name, Genoan, changed by American pronunciation, became the term we use today, "jeans."

What is an *anemometer*?
It is an instrument used to measure the speed of the wind.

Who was *Atahualpa*?
He was a sixteenth century Inca king captured by Pizarro. In exchange for his freedom, Atahualpa agreed to give Pizarro a room full of gold, but after he paid him, Pizarro had him strangled.

What is an *atoll*?
It is a ring-shaped coral island which encloses a lagoon. Atolls are found in the tropics in the Pacific and Indian oceans.

What is the *aurora polaris*?
Aurora polaris or "polar light" is a phenomenon of light that occurs in magnetic storms. It fills the skies in the polar regions with lively moving colors. The colors form shapes such as arches, bands, columns or even crowns.

What does *self-taught* mean?
We call someone self-taught when that person has learned everything by himself, without the help of a teacher or school. They obtain knowledge through life experiences and from reading.

What was the *first plastic*?
The first plastic was invented in 1906 by a Belgian chemist, Baekeland. It was called bakelite and was used as an electric insulator and for the production of electric sockets and switches.

What is the *deepest lake* in the world?
Lake Baikal in southern Siberia, the Soviet Union is the deepest lake known to man. It measures 5,712 feet deep.

What is an *ice-floe*?
It is a layer of floating ice covering the polar seas. It forms when the temperature of the sea water reaches twenty eight degrees Fahrenheit.

Who invented the game of *dice*?
We do not know the exact person who invented this game because dice have been found all over throughout history. Today's cube-shaped dice, however, come from Mesopotamia. Some dice found consist of clay while others are made of stone. Some dice clearly intended for cheating have even been found.

Where did *robots* get their name?
The word "robot" comes from the Czechoslovak word "robota," meaning "compulsory labor." Robots were invented to do the tasks that people do not like to do because they are too repetitive or tiring. Today robots truly have "artificial intelligence" and are able to do a wide range of tasks.

What is an *astrolabe* used for?

The astrolabe is an ancient scientific instrument. It was probably invented by the Greek astronomer, Hipparchus, in the second century, B.C. It was used to determine the position of the stars by measuring their height on the horizon. It can also calculate the time of sunrise or sunset.

What does *BASIC* mean?

BASIC stands for Beginner's All-purpose Symbolic Instruction Code. It is the language employed for the programming of computers and electronic calculators. BASIC is relatively easy to learn and is widely used with calculators and personal computers.

Who were the *Beatles*?

The Beatles were a famous English rock group who were extremely popular around the world during the 1960s. The four members were George Harrison, John Lennon, Paul McCartney and Ringo Starr.

What is a *best-seller*?

It is a very popular book. A book becomes a best-seller when it sells more copies than any other book during a particular week.

When was the *bicycle* invented?

The bicycle was invented around the end of the last century. Its ancestors were two-wheeled vehicles without pedals. The rider pushed them along with his feet. Some early examples were the "celerifere" from 1690 and the "draisine" from 1818. In 1855 Ernest and Pierre Michaux invented the bicycle. It had pedals attached to the rear wheel, which was much bigger than the front wheel. Our bicycle today is based on this early model.

What is the *big bang* theory?

It is a theory about the origin of the universe. It states that the universe was the result of an explosion of a mass of extremely hot dense matter. As the fragments cooled they formed the planets, the sun and satellites.

Who was *Buffalo Bill*?

He was an American adventurer who lived in the last century. His real name was William Frederick Cody. His nickname came from his skill as a buffalo hunter. He took part in expeditions against the Sioux Indians and later formed a circus.

Where do we get *cinnamon* from?

Cinnamon comes from the dry bark of the cinnamon tree that grows in Asia. Because of its special flavor and aroma, it is used in cooking, in perfume-making and even in medicine.

What kinds of *toys* did children play with in the past?

The most common toys in ancient times were rattles and stone, clay or bone figures. In Egypt, wooden dolls with movable arms have been found. Also found there was a crocodile, dating back to 1,600 B.C., with a mouth that opened and closed!

How many *bones* are there in our body?

When we are born, our bodies have about 350 bones but when we become adults, we have less. As we grow, some of our bones fuse with others. This is why the adult skeleton has only 206 bones. Some people, however, have a few extra bones in their tendons. They are called sesamoid bones. The only sesamoid bone we all have is the patella, a bone in our knee.

When did the *first maps* appear?

By the time of the ancient Egyptians and Babylonians in 3,000 B.C. maps already existed. They were used for navigation and to show the boundaries of property. The Egyptians, in particular, needed to indicate on their maps the size and shape of their fields because the Nile River flooded periodically and covered the ground with a thick mud that carried away all other reference points.

Is it true that an *octopus* can change color?

If we tap the side of an aquarium which has an octopus living inside, we will see him turn pale. Experiments show that the octopus changes color when he is surprised or angry.

Do *whales* really sing?

If you were to suspend a microphone deep into the ocean in certain places you would be able to hear the extraordinary, unforgettable sounds of a whale "song." These enormous mammals cannot communicate by signs, because it is impossible to see very far below the surface of the ocean. Instead, they use sounds to communicate. Their songs, which sound like electronic music, can tell other whales where to find food. Whales also "sing" when looking for a mate.

Will the *sun* ever burn out?

Indeed the sun will burn out, but not for a long time. Scientists estimate that the sun is already four billion years old but it still has a long way to go before it burns itself out.

Only when all the hydrogen that the sun contains is changed to helium will we need to worry. That should not happen for at least another forty billion years.

How old is the *first stamp*?

The first stamp was printed in England in 1840. It was a black stamp with the image of Queen Victoria on it and was worth one penny. A Scotsman, Rowland Hill, invented it.

Which is the world's *biggest waterfall*?

Angel Falls in Venezuela is the tallest waterfall. It has a drop of 3,212 feet. The water falls from such a great height that it turns into a cloud-like mist. Because the wind carries the water and showers the nearby countryside, the rain forests around it are very dense and luxurious.

What kind of *fish* changes shape to defend itself?

The porcupine fish, or blowfish, defends itself by changing its shape. When it is attacked, it does not try to escape. Instead, it blows itself up until it looks like a little balloon full of sharp spines. The change in size frightens its attacker. If the enlarged shape does not scare the other fish, the spines, which normally lie flat, usually do.

What is *kaolin*?
Kaolin, or china clay, is a white or greyish-yellow clay that is used to make porcelain.

Who was *Al Capone*?
He was an American gangster from Chicago. In the 1920s he profited in the illegal sale of alcohol.

What is *carding*?
It is an operation in which fibers like cotton and wool are "combed." This is done with a machine that has rolls with teeth on them that separate and clean the fibers.

What is a *food chain*?
A food chain is the way in which materials and energy circulate in the natural world. The first "ring" of a chain are plants, which are eaten by herbivores or grazing animals. Then carnivores or meat-eaters eat the grazers and other carnivores. What is left after they have finished eating, is broken down by fungi and bacteria and returned to the soil. New plants grow in the soil and the cycle starts all over again.

When was *baseball* invented?
Games using balls and bats have existed for many years. Early forms of baseball went by different names so the exact date of baseball's origin is not known. We do know that the first organized games were played in New York in 1845.

What is *freeze-drying*?
It is a technique used to preserve foods. It works by eliminating all the water from a food, dehydrating it. However, it does not completely change the food. If it is soaked in water, its original properties are restored.

Does the *edelweiss* come from the Alps?
Although we usually associate Switzerland's national flower with the Alps, it actually originated in Asia and the Ural Mountains. It migrated to the west as far as the Pyrenees during the last ice age. Today it is common all over the Alps.

Are there any *worms* as big as snakes?
In certain tropical countries, there are worms that are truly exceptional. In Australia there are some worms that are nine feet long.

Is there really a *bat* which lives on fish?
Yes, there is a bat in the American tropics which supplements its diet with fish. About four inches long, this bat catches fish at night. It drags its claws just beneath the surface of the water. When it discovers a fish, it dips its tail in the water and the fish jumps out. Then it flicks the fish in the air with the membrane that stretches between its tail and back feet and grabs it with its strong curved claws.

What is *acupuncture*?
It is a therapeutic treatment practiced in China since ancient times. It consists of inserting very fine needles into the body in certain places. These places, according to the theory, circulate vital energy. Today, acupuncture is also beginning to be used in our hospitals to relieve pain.

What is a *diamond* made of?
It is a mineral made of pure carbon in its crystal form. The diamond is a precious stone, usually having no color. When cut correctly, it reflects the light in a beautiful way. Diamond is also the hardest material in the world. The Kohinoor Diamond is one of the most beautiful diamonds in existence.

How does the *spitting spider* catch his prey?
Of all the many techniques animals have for hunting, one of the strangest is that of the spitting spider. This spider catches small insects by attacking them from a distance with carefully aimed spit. The saliva quickly solidifies into sticky strings that entangle the body of the prey, immobilizing it. Then all the spider has to do is eat it.

What is a *tuning fork* for?
A tuning fork is a small steel instrument shaped like a fork. When tapped, it always provides the same note, "la." Musicians use it as a reference in order to tune their instruments.

What is the *smallest mammal*?
The smallest mammal is the shrew, some of which are less than two inches long, excluding the tail. It can be found all over the world, except in the polar regions, Australia, New Zealand, Greenland and Tasmania.

Did people living in the New World in ancient times ever play *ball games*?
Yes, Indians who lived around Vera Cruz, Mexico from three hundred – nine hundred A.D. played a ritual ball game called tlachtli. There are still ruins of their ball courts in existence today and it is believed that the game sometimes included human sacrifices.

What is the *muezzin*?
In the Islamic faith, the muezzin is the man who calls the faithful to prayer. He does this five times a day from the top of a minaret.

What is the *Pentagon*?
It is the building in Arlington, Virginia where the Department of Defense is located. Its name comes from its shape which is in the form of a pentagon.

What events make up the *decathalon*?
The one hundred meter dash, the long jump, the shot-put, the high jump, the four hundred meter run, the 110 meter high hurdles, the discus throw, the pole vault, the javelin throw and the 1,500 meter run constitute the decathalon.

What is a *mikado*?
It is a Japanese word that literally means "honorable gate," referring to the imperial palace. It was a title of a Japanese emperor.

Where does the *Dead Sea* get its name?
The Dead Sea is a very big saltwater lake located 1,296 feet below sea level. It is located along the border between Israel and Jordan. It was given this name because no plants or animals can live in its salty water.

Why was the *National Park System* started?
National parks are huge tracts of land protected by the law. The system was set up to conserve natural scenery and wildlife and also places of historic interest. There are over 131,800 square miles of national parks in the United States. The biggest is Denali National Park in Alaska; the smallest is Hot Springs, Arkansas.

What is a *troika*?

A troika is a Russian sleigh drawn by three horses side by side. It is used in the winter to ride over the snow.

Where is the *Wailing Wall*?

It is in the eastern part of Jerusalem, occupied since 1967 by the Israelis. The Wailing Wall is the last remaining part of a temple destroyed by the Roman emperor Titus in 70, A.D. It is a place of prayer for Jews.

What are *castanets*?

They are a percussion instrument made of two small pieces of wood, hollowed out like shells. Clicked together by moving the fingers, they produce a short, sharp sound.

Who invented *ink*?

The ancient Egyptians were already using ink five thousand years ago. They used black ink for their texts and red ink for titles, punctuation and for the sum of accounts. In China, ink was invented in the third century, A.D. by Wei Tan.

When did the *first camera* appear in stores?

In 1888 George Eastman perfected the Kodak camera. In 1892 he established the Eastman Kodak Company in Rochester, New York, where he began to mass-produce cameras and films.

How many miles are there in a *light year*?

A light year is the distance that light can travel in one year. This corresponds to 5,880,000,000,000 miles.

What does *WWF* stand for?

WWF stands for World Wildlife Fund. It is an international organization founded in 1961 to protect all kinds of wildlife. Its mascot is the panda.

Where do *yaks* live?

Yaks, which belong to the bovine family, are found throughout the high Central Asian steppes. The domestic yak of Tibet is raised as a work animal and is valued for its hair, skin, meat and milk.

INDEX

190